Jonah:
A Study in
Greatness

Jonah: A Study in Greatness

Dr. Bo Wagner

Word of His Mouth Publishers
Mooresboro, NC

All Scripture quotations are taken from the **King James Version** of the Bible.

ISBN: 978-1-941039-09-0
Printed in the United States of America
©2019 Dr. Bo Wagner

Word of His Mouth Publishers
Mooresboro, NC 28114
www.wordofhismouth.com

Table of Contents

Chapter   Page

Introduction 1
1   A Study in Great Wickedness 3
2   A Study in Great Waywardness 17
3   A Study in Great Windiness............................27
4   A Study in Great Wondering...........................37
5   A Study in Great Wretchedness 47
6   A Study in Great Wisdom 59
7   A Study in Great Will Breaking.....................71
8   A Study in Great Wastefulness 85
9   A Study in Great Willingness.........................97
10   A Study in Great Wrong...............................109
11   A Study in Great Worthiness 119
Works Cited...127

Introduction

Frustrating. Filled with potential. Petulant. Powerful. Deceptive. Repentant. All of these phrases and many more describe the man Jonah, one of the most paradoxical men to ever cross the pages of Holy Writ. This man led the single greatest evangelistic campaign in all of human history and yet was miserable at the results!

Everyone knows that, according to the Bible, Jonah was swallowed by a great fish. But if that is all we know of the man and the book, we truly are missing the most important parts of both.

It is my prayer that through this humble effort to expound the book of Jonah verse by verse to my readers, they may learn of Jonah, yes, but even more so that they may learn of the God of Jonah. Jonah may have been a great rebel, but God was and is an even greater Savior. It is in His honor that I present to you this little book.

Bo Wagner

Chapter One
A Study in Great Wickedness

Jonah 1:1 *Now the word of the LORD came unto Jonah the son of Amittai, saying,* **2** *Arise, go to Nineveh, that great city, and cry against it; for their wickedness is come up before me.*

The book of Jonah is one of the most marked, ridiculed, targeted books in the Bible. Preacher gets a call from God...Preacher runs from God... Preacher ends up on a boat...A gigantic storm threatens to capsize the boat...Preacher gets thrown overboard...Preacher gets swallowed up by giant fish and manages to live inside the fish's belly for three days and gets vomited out onto land and lives to preach about it.

The hater of God and the critic of Scripture could find the book of Jonah in a Bible drill faster than probably every single member of any church anywhere.

But all they seem to know about it is the miraculous account of Jonah in the whale's belly. And that one thing that they do know about it is enough, for them, to make the entire book unworthy of belief.

3

Not only is that part of the book entirely true, every other part of the book is true as well. What you are reading about in the book of Jonah is not an allegory or a myth or a legend; it is actual history. And it is not simply a fish tale, it is actually a study in greatness, both for good and for bad. Let me show you why I say that:

Jonah 1:2 *Arise, go to Nineveh, that **great** city, and cry against it; for their wickedness is come up before me.*

Jonah 1:4 *But the LORD sent out a **great** wind into the sea, and there was a mighty tempest in the sea, so that the ship was like to be broken.*

Jonah 1:12 *And he said unto them, Take me up, and cast me forth into the sea; so shall the sea be calm unto you: for I know that for my sake this **great** tempest is upon you.*

Jonah 1:17 *Now the LORD had prepared a **great** fish to swallow up Jonah. And Jonah was in the belly of the fish three days and three nights.*

Jonah 3:2 *Arise, go unto Nineveh, that **great** city, and preach unto it the preaching that I bid thee.*

Jonah 3:3 *So Jonah arose, and went unto Nineveh, according to the word of the LORD. Now Nineveh was an exceeding **great** city of three days' journey.*

Jonah 4:2 *And he prayed unto the LORD, and said, I pray thee, O LORD, was not this my saying, when I was yet in my country? Therefore I fled before unto Tarshish: for I knew that thou art a gracious God, and merciful, slow to anger, and of **great** kindness, and repentest thee of the evil.*

Jonah 4:11 *And should not I spare Nineveh, that **great** city, wherein are more than sixscore thousand* *persons that cannot discern between their right hand and their left hand; and also much cattle?*

Eight times in four very short chapters, we find the word great mentioned. And even when it is not mentioned, it is implied a great many more times.

The book of Jonah is not about a fish; the book of Jonah is about a great God who had great plans and was willing to go to great lengths to show great mercy to great sinners. The book of Jonah is the missionary book of the Old Testament and the visual prophecy of the fact that God was going to bring Gentiles into the fold of salvation.

So, we are going to study our way through the book of Jonah. Yes, there will be a great fish, but that is actually such a small part of the story. As the chapter heading indicates, we will begin by looking at A Study in Great Wickedness.

The call

Jonah 1:1 *Now the word of the LORD came unto Jonah the son of Amittai...*

As the book of Jonah opens, the man for whom the book is named is mentioned. You might want to know that from the earliest days of the canon of the Old Testament, it was nearly unanimously accepted that Jonah himself was the author of this book. And as you read the text itself, you will come, I believe, to that exact same conclusion. Jonah speaks extensively in the first person, especially in his prayer of chapter two.

Names in the Bible are normally loaded with meaning, and Jonah is no exception. His name means "dove." That name, though, does not seem at all to match his character as shown in this book. Jonah is anything but peaceful and gentle throughout these four chapters.

It is one thing to have an illustrious name; it is quite another thing to deserve that name. Had Jonah even a measure of dove-like quality to go along with his passion and power, he would have arrived at Nineveh sooner, rejoiced in the results, and likely stayed around for quite a while to disciple those who had come to trust under the wings of his God.

Jonah's father was a man named Amittai. His name means "truth." Amittai is only mentioned twice in the Bible, and both times it is in the context of being the father of Jonah.

But Jonah, regarded as one of the "minor" prophets, is mentioned nineteen times in the Old Testament, and seven times in the New Testament where his name is spelled Jonas. Those seven times he is mentioned in the New Testament all came from the lips of none other than the Lord Jesus Christ Himself.

Do you remember what we said the book of Jonah is a study in? It is a study in greatness. I showed you all of the usages of the word great in this book and told you that it is implied a great many more times. But now let me show you something else:

Matthew 12:41 *The men of Nineveh shall rise in judgment with this generation, and shall condemn it: because they repented at the preaching of Jonas; and, behold, a **greater** than Jonas is here.*

Jesus Himself gave testimony to the greatness of Jonah. He compared Himself to Jonah and said that He was greater than Jonah. Had Jonah not been an incredibly great man in everyone's estimation during the days of Christ, the Lord would never have made that comparison. And making this all the more impressive is the fact that Jonah lived around eight hundred fifty years before Christ!

If I asked you to name a great person from eight hundred fifty years ago, I am guessing that every one of you would draw a blank and sit there staring at this book silently.

But everyone in the days of Christ looked back nearly one thousand years and acknowledged the greatness of Jonah.

Now let me tell you something else about Jonah that I am guessing very few Christians even know. The book of Jonah is not even the first place we read about Jonah in the Bible. There was more to Jonah's ministry than just this one event of going to Nineveh to preach.

2 Kings 14:23 *In the fifteenth year of Amaziah the son of Joash king of Judah Jeroboam the son of Joash king of Israel began to reign in Samaria, and reigned forty and one years.* **24** *And he did that which was evil in the sight of the LORD: he departed not from all the sins of Jeroboam the son of Nebat, who made Israel to sin.* **25** *He restored the coast of Israel from the entering of Hamath unto the sea of the plain, according to the word of the LORD God of Israel,* **which he spake by the hand of his servant Jonah,** *the son of Amittai, the prophet, which was of Gathhepher.*

Let me give you the back story to this passage and then explain the passage itself. When you understand this,

7

it will shed new light on just how very wrong Jonah was in how he behaved in the book that bears his name.

There are two Jeroboams mentioned in the verses we just read. In verse twenty-four, we read of Jeroboam, the son of Nebat. He was the first king of the northern tribes after the civil war that split Israel in two. Rehoboam, the son of Solomon, caused the civil war by being an absolute brat and bully. So, the ten tribes of the north split off and called themselves Israel. Two tribes remained in the south and called themselves Judah.

Years later, another Jeroboam had come to the throne. This Jeroboam was wicked, just like the first one. Both Jeroboams and the nation that followed them deserved nothing but God's judgment and wrath. They brought idolatry into the land, they made alliances with wicked people, and they refused to seek after God.

But the second king Jeroboam, mentioned in verse twenty-three, presided over one of the most prosperous and wealthy periods in all of the history of the nation of Israel. And during his reign, at some point, God sent Jonah the prophet to see him. Jonah prophesied that some of the territories that Israel had lost to their enemies during previous years were going to be regained during the reign of Jeroboam II.

And it happened just like Jonah said. So God sent Jonah to a wicked king who ruled over wicked people and gave him a prophecy of God being merciful and gracious to them. And Jonah doubtless was thrilled to take that message to him! Remember that when Jonah is unhappy with a message, he does not hesitate to let everybody know that fact. But when he is told to take this message of grace and mercy to a wicked king over wicked people, he utters not a single word of protest.

And yet some years later when God tells him to take another message of potential mercy and grace to another king and another wicked people, suddenly Jonah protests with all his might. In fact, he goes so far as to defy God and refuse to take that message.

Isn't the problem pretty obvious? The first message of mercy and grace to an undeserving people was sent to the Jews; the second message of mercy and grace to an undeserving people was sent to Gentiles. Among other things, Jonah was eaten up with racial pride. And how ironic is it that in his day it was bigotry from the Jews toward the Gentiles, and in our day Gentiles often react in that same type of bigotry and pride toward the Jews?

Now, yes, as we will see in just a little bit, there was at least one other aspect to it, the cruelty of the Assyrians and the knowledge that they were at some point going to conquer Israel. But there is little to no doubt that Jonah was acting just like most every other one of his countrymen would have acted when told to take a message of mercy and grace the Gentiles. The Jews were willing to follow God up to a point, but that, to them, was "crossing the line."

But for now, remember what we have in the text. The call of God has come to one of His servants, the prophet Jonah from Gathhepher, a region of Galilee.

The corruption

Jonah 1:1 *Now the word of the LORD came unto Jonah the son of Amittai, saying, 2 Arise, go to Nineveh,*

9

that great city, and cry against it; for their wickedness is come up before me.

In the first verse of this book, we are introduced to the first of the two central characters, Jonah the prophet. In the second verse of this book, we are introduced to the second of the two central characters, a city by the name of Nineveh and the people of that city.

What God said in verse two in just a few short words will begin to open our eyes to what was going on in the heart of Jonah.

When God called Jonah to go to Nineveh, He was calling him to go to what was then the largest city in the entire world; He was asking him to go to the city that was regarded as the capital of the Gentile world. If there was no Washington DC., no Chicago, no Los Angeles, no Paris, no Rome, no Moscow, if all of the great cities of our world were gone except for New York City, then you would have some sense of the importance of Nineveh. If all of those other cities were gone, the world would literally revolve around New York. And during the time period of the life of Jonah, the world very much revolved around the city known as Nineveh.

Nineveh was the capital of the Assyrian Empire. This was an ancient people with a great deal of history and a large legacy. Let me show you just how far back Nineveh went:

Genesis 10:8 *And Cush begat Nimrod: he began to be a mighty one in the earth.* **9** *He was a mighty hunter before the LORD: wherefore it is said, Even as Nimrod the mighty hunter before the LORD.* **10** *And the beginning of his kingdom was Babel, and Erech, and Accad, and*

Calneh, in the land of Shinar. **11** *Out of that land went forth Asshur, and builded* **Nineveh**, *and the city Rehoboth, and Calah,*

The city of Nineveh was built shortly after the great flood of Noah's day and right before God separated mankind into different languages and peoples at the tower of Babel. And though the man Asshur here is mentioned as the builder of Nineveh, according to Micah the prophet it was actually Nimrod that was the driving force behind the building of all of Assyria including Nineveh:

Micah 5:6 *And they shall waste the land of Assyria with the sword, and the land of Nimrod in the entrances thereof: thus shall he deliver us from the Assyrian, when he cometh into our land, and when he treadeth within our borders.*

Nineveh was an old city started by a very wicked man who was the leader of the rebellion against God before the Tower of Babel. And for all of their history, Assyria walked in that pathway. They were forever the enemies of God and of God's people.

As to the city itself, it was roughly sixty miles in circumference. The walls were one hundred feet high and wide enough for three chariots to race side by side on. It had 1,500 high towers on those walls. The population is estimated to have been between one and two million people. (Feinberg, 143)

Here is another stunning fact. Though Assyria never dominated the world as thoroughly as the Chaldeans did with their great capital city of Babylon, the city of Nineveh was actually substantially bigger than the great city of Babylon!

Nineveh was bordered by three large rivers. It was a near-perfect situation for growing a wide variety of produce. They had apples and palm trees. Figs and olives. Pomegranates, almonds, mulberries, even cotton. So they had all the water and all of the food they could ever have wished for.

They also had money, lots of it. Nineveh was a center of world commerce. They traded in silver and copper and bronze, horses and, cedarwood. They produced and dealt in art and glass.

But the main number one industry of Nineveh and all of Assyria was war.

This was a military kingdom. For a very long time, they were one of the worst scourges of earth. They had so very many soldiers that they had to keep going to war just to pay them and feed them. And it was that propensity for war among other things that was doubtless weighing on Jonah's mind when the call came from God to go to Nineveh. You see, another prophet had already given a word from the Lord about Assyria and what they were going to do to Israel:

Hosea 9:1 *Rejoice not, O Israel, for joy, as other people: for thou hast gone a whoring from thy God, thou hast loved a reward upon every cornfloor.* **2** *The floor and the winepress shall not feed them, and the new wine shall fail in her.* **3** *They shall not dwell in the LORD'S land; but Ephraim shall return to Egypt, and* ***they shall eat unclean things in Assyria.***

This was a prophecy that Israel was going to go into captivity to Assyria. And every Jew knew that nothing good ever happened with any interactions with the Assyrians. Let me give you a passage from a history site that describes it pretty well:

"The Assyrian war machine was the most efficient military force in the ancient world up until the fall of the empire in 612 BCE. The secret to its success was a professionally trained standing army, iron weapons, advanced engineering skills, effective tactics, and, most importantly, a complete ruthlessness which came to characterize the Assyrians to their neighbors and subjects and still attaches itself to the reputation of Assyria in the modern day. A phrase oft-repeated by Assyrian kings in their inscriptions regarding military conquests is 'I destroyed, devastated, and burned with fire' those cities, towns, and regions which resisted Assyrian rule.

"The Assyrian kings were not to be trifled with and their inscriptions vividly depict the fate which was certain for those who defied them. The historian Simon Anglim writes:

"The Assyrians created the world's first great army and the world's first great empire. This was held together by two factors: their superior abilities in siege warfare and their reliance on sheer, unadulterated terror. It was Assyrian policy always to demand that examples be made of those who resisted them; this included deportations of entire peoples and horrific physical punishments. One inscription from a temple in the city of Nimrod recorded the fate of the leaders of the city of Suru on the Euphrates River, who rebelled from and were reconquered by, King Ashurbanipal:

" 'I built a pillar at the city gate and I flayed all the chief men who had revolted and I covered the pillar with their skins; some I walled up inside the pillar, some I impaled upon the pillar on stakes.'

"Such punishments were not uncommon. Furthermore, inscriptions recording these vicious acts of retribution were displayed throughout the empire to serve as a warning." (Mark, 2018)

These were the Assyrians. They skinned people alive. They walled people up inside of pillars and left them in there to die. They impaled people on stakes. They did all of this publicly and visibly so that everyone would know what they were like.

Jonah knew what they were like. Jonah knew what Israel was in for if Assyria survived and came against them.

But Jonah was not the only one who knew what the Assyrians were like. Look at verse two of our text again, and noticed that God knew what they were like:

Jonah 1:2 *Arise, go to Nineveh, that great city, and cry against it; for their wickedness is come up before me.*

God told Jonah that the wickedness of Nineveh had "come up before him." The only thing He ever said remotely like that in the Bible was in describing Sodom and Gomorrah:

Genesis 18:20 *And the LORD said, Because the cry of Sodom and Gomorrah is great, and because their sin is very grievous;* **21** *I will go down now, and see whether they have done altogether according to the cry of it,* ***which is come unto me;*** *and if not, I will know.*

Cities like Sodom and Gomorrah and Nineveh were in a league of their own when it came to wickedness. This was not just your average garden-variety wickedness; this was wickedness that had so captured the attention of the God of heaven that He was going to send a man with a warning that they only had forty days of life left before He destroyed them all. That is some very, very serious evil. This truly was a great wickedness.

What I am really captured by, though, is how very different God and Jonah reacted to that great wickedness. Please understand that God knew the wickedness of Nineveh and the Assyrians far better than even Jonah did. And yet, God wanted to send a prophet to them with the message of warning, and the prophet wanted to leave them to perish without any warning.

I wonder how often it is like that even today? I wonder how often God in heaven looks at some of the most vile and wicked people with a look of mercy on His face, while we, His people, are looking at those exact same wicked people with a look of anger and judgment our faces?

God knows the wickedness of this world even better than we do. And if He is willing to extend mercy and grace to a wicked world, the best thing we can do is rejoice in that and even help to spread the message, seeing as how He redeemed us out of that exact same wickedness that the world is still in. Jesus Christ came to die for the sins of this wicked, horrible, violent world. And now, just like then, God is looking at His people and saying, "Go give them the message that I have for them. Go tell them that they are wicked and heading for destruction, but I have made a way for them to be saved..."

Chapter Two
A Study in Great Waywardness

Jonah 1:3 *But Jonah rose up to flee unto Tarshish from the presence of the LORD, and went down to Joppa; and he found a ship going to Tarshish: so he paid the fare thereof, and went down into it, to go with them unto Tarshish from the presence of the LORD.*

A planned destination

Jonah 1:3 *But Jonah rose up to flee unto Tarshish from the presence of the LORD, and went down to Joppa; and he found a ship going to Tarshish: so he paid the fare thereof, and went down into it, to go with them unto Tarshish from the presence of the LORD.*

You should remember from our study of the first two verses where it was that God commissioned Jonah to go:

Jonah 1:1 *Now the word of the LORD came unto Jonah the son of Amittai, saying,* **2** *Arise, go to* **Nineveh**, *that great city, and cry against it; for their wickedness is come up before me.*

Nineveh. The capital city of the Assyrian empire. The then-current scourge of the earth. The people who were not only cruel but open about it and proud of it.

As we observed in the first chapter, when God called Jonah to go to Nineveh, He was calling him to go to what was then the largest city in the entire world. He was asking him to go to the city that was regarded as the capital of the Gentile world. If there was no Washington DC, no Chicago, no Los Angeles, no Paris, no Rome, no Moscow, if all of the great cities of our world were gone except for New York City, then you would have some sense of the importance of Nineveh. If all of those other cities were gone, the world would literally revolve around New York. And during the time period of the life of Jonah, the world very much revolved around the city known as Nineveh.

As to the city itself, it was roughly sixty miles in circumference. The walls were one hundred feet high and wide enough for three chariots to race side by side on. It had 1,500 high towers on those walls. The population is estimated to have been around two million people. It was the biggest city in the world, by a long shot.

All of that you know. But what you do not yet know is the geographical location of the city of Ninevah. And it makes a difference in multiple ways.

Nineveh was located in what in our day would be northern Iraq. Ninevah was approximately five hundred fifty miles inland, to the east of Israel. That is where God told Jonah to go. Instead, Jonah determined to go to Tarshish, which was in what is now modern-day Spain. Tarshish was approximately 2,100 miles to the west of

Israel. God told Jonah to go east to Ninevah; Jonah determined to go west till he was 2,650 miles away from Ninevah. 2,650 miles. And do you know why he settled for a location 2,650 miles away? Because it was literally as far as he could go in the exact opposite direction! He could not go any farther without swimming; Spain is on the Atlantic Ocean, and not many, if any at all, in those days knew that there was actually anything on the other side of that.

Two thousand six hundred fifty miles. That is not a tiny bit of disobedience; that is "selling the entire farm" disobedience. Jonah is leaving the ministry; Jonah is leaving God. Jonah is throwing it all away to make sure that Ninevah does not have a potentially soul-saving message from God. So, the first way his planned destination makes a difference is that it was as far as he could possibly go to get out of taking the message to Nineveh.

The second way his planned destination makes a difference is that when the fish spit him out on land three days after swallowing him, it did not spit him out in Nineveh. In order to accomplish that, it would have had to circle the entire African continent and cover 15,000 miles in three days' time, going from the Atlantic Ocean through the Indian Ocean in the process.

That fish, if it spat him out in the closest possible location to Nineveh, would have had to spit him out right where he left port.

And with the heart of God on this subject, with his desire to rescue hundreds of thousands of souls in Nineveh, you know that is exactly what happened.

And so Jonah later did go to Nineveh; but to do so, he had to cross every single inch of ground he would have crossed if he had been obedient to begin with, only now he had to cross it after having spent three days in the belly of the fish. That fact will most certainly come in to play later on in the account.

A point of departure

Jonah 1:3 *But Jonah rose up to flee unto Tarshish from the presence of the LORD,* **and went down to Joppa; and he found a ship going to Tarshish***: so he paid the fare thereof, and went down into it, to go with them unto Tarshish from the presence of the LORD.*

Jonah's point of departure on his intended trip to Tarshish was the city of Joppa. That city is still in existence today, only now it goes by the name of Jaffa. As long as it has been inhabited, it has been used as a seaport, and it still is today. The Bible itself gives testimony to that fact repeatedly:

2 Chronicles 2:16 *And we will cut wood out of Lebanon, as much as thou shalt need: and we will bring it to thee in floats by sea to Joppa; and thou shalt carry it up to Jerusalem.*

Ezra 3:7 *They gave money also unto the masons, and to the carpenters; and meat, and drink, and oil, unto them of Zidon, and to them of Tyre, to bring cedar trees from Lebanon to the sea of Joppa, according to the grant that they had of Cyrus king of Persia.*

Acts 10:32 *Send therefore to Joppa, and call hither Simon, whose surname is Peter; he is lodged in the house* *of one Simon a tanner by the sea side: who, when he cometh, shall speak unto thee.*

Jonah went to Joppa because he knew he could find seaworthy vessels there, ships that could take him a very, very long way away from God, or so he thought. He was going to find out the hard way that there is no such vessel anywhere.

A payment of disobedience

Jonah 1:3 *But Jonah rose up to flee unto Tarshish from the presence of the LORD, and went down to Joppa; and he found a ship going to Tarshish:* **so he paid the fare thereof**, *and went down into it, to go with them unto Tarshish from the presence of the LORD.*

When God commanded Jonah to go to Nineveh, what command did He give that concerned Jonah's wallet? None, absolutely none. God did not tell Jonah to pay his way to Nineveh. He just told him to go.

But when Jonah determined to go to Tarshish, we find him opening his own wallet and pulling out his own money to pay the fare aboard that ship. In other words, Jonah's disobedience was literally costing him.

People may not realize it, but disobedience to God always costs them.

David did not think so when he cast lustful eyes on to Bathsheba, but if you could have gone to him a few years later and asked after his family was destroyed and his reputation in tatters, he would have said, "There is a cost for disobeying God..."

Moses did not think so when he struck the rock in anger, but if you could have gone to him a few years later

21

and asked as he looked over into the Promised Land but was not allowed to go in, he would have said, "There is a cost for disobeying God..."

Samson did not think so when he laid his head in Delilah's lap, but if you could have gone to him a few years later and asked as he blindly ground for his captors, he would have said, "There is a cost for disobeying God..."

Judas did not think so when he betrayed Christ, but if you could have gone to him a few years later and asked as he screamed from the flames of hell, he would have said, "There is a cost for disobeying God..."

You may sock all of your money away in CDs, put all of your valuable possessions in an impregnable safe, put bars on your windows, and have the most technologically advanced alarm system in the history of mankind, but you will never escape the fact that there is a cost for disobeying God.

And by the way, sadly, you will not be the only one to pay that cost.

Jonah had to travel from Galilee to Joppa, then set sail, and got who knows how far out into the Mediterranean, then was swallowed by the fish, and spent three days in his belly, then got spit out onto dry land. He very likely wasted three weeks to a month before he even got back to the starting line of his journey.

Do you think for even a moment that out of a city of two million people nobody died during the months that Jonah was late getting there? I believe the Bible is very clear that Jonah was saved and is in heaven, but how much blood did he have on his hands when he got there? How many people died and went to hell because God's man was not there to give the message when he was supposed to be there? Of all the things people disobey God in, this has got to be the worst. Not just preachers; the Great Commission is for all of us. Every child of God is called to be a soul-winner. And if you are expecting a pastor to be the only soul winner in your church, you are creating a horrible paradigm. You see, there will be people that you know and meet that your pastor will never know and meet! If a person must be won by a pastor, then a great many people will end up in hell simply because they never heard. But if every child of God acts as a soul winner, no one needs to go without hearing.

There is going to be a cost for any time we sin by refusing to fulfill the Great Commission, but we will not be the only ones to pay that cost.

A purpose declared

Jonah 1:3 *But Jonah rose up to flee unto Tarshish* **from the presence of the LORD***, and went down to Joppa; and he found a ship going to Tarshish: so he paid the fare thereof, and went down into it, to go with them unto Tarshish* **from the presence of the LORD***.*

It is not a mistake or an example of careless writing that there is a phrase repeated word for word in this verse. This was not produced by the Department of Redundancy Department. Twice, the Bible tells us that Jonah's purpose for going to Tarshish was to flee from the presence of the Lord. Jonah was trying to get away from the presence of God.

Do you understand what that means? Jonah, Jonah the prophet, did not understand the nature of the God he had been called to serve.

It is ironic that a prophet did not understand the nature of God when a politician did:

Psalm 139:1 *O LORD, thou hast searched me, and known me.* **2** *Thou knowest my downsitting and mine uprising, thou understandest my thought afar off.* **3** *Thou compassest my path and my lying down, and art acquainted with all my ways.* **4** *For there is not a word in my tongue, but, lo, O LORD, thou knowest it altogether.* **5** *Thou hast beset me behind and before, and laid thine hand upon me.* **6** *Such knowledge is too wonderful for me; it is high, I cannot attain unto it.* **7** *Whither shall I go from thy spirit? or* **whither shall I flee from thy presence?** **8** *If I ascend up into heaven, thou art there: if I make my bed in hell, behold, thou art there.* **9** *If I take the wings of the morning, and dwell in the uttermost parts of the sea;* **10** *Even there shall thy hand lead me, and thy right hand shall hold me.*

King David, the politician, understood the omnipresence of God when Jonah, the prophet, apparently did not! And what makes this even sadder is that the Psalm that we just read was actually available to Jonah to read in his day.

If you are planning on running from the presence of God, please allow me to make you aware of the fact that doing so is an impossibility.

You can run from the will of God.

You can run from the blessings of God.

But you cannot ever, anywhere, in any way run from the presence of God.

If you come to church, you are in the presence of God.

If you lay out of church, you are in the presence of God.

While you are being faithful to your spouse, you are in the presence of God.

While you are committing adultery or fornication, you are in the presence of God.

While you are hungrily looking at your Bible, you are in the presence of God.

While you are lustfully looking at pornography, you are in the presence of God.

While you are listening to songs that glorify God, you are in the presence of God.

While you are listening to songs that blaspheme God and use filthy language and encourage you to all manner of sin, you are in the presence of God.

While you are hanging around good Christian friends who encourage you to righteousness, you are in the presence of God.

While you are hanging around reprobate heathens who hate God and love wickedness and are drawing you into their sin, you are in the presence of God.

You can choose to do right, or you can choose to do wrong, but you cannot choose to do either of those things privately. Whatever you do, you are in the presence of God, and He sees and knows it all.

This was a great waywardness on the part of Jonah in so many ways.

It was a waywardness that almost certainly allowed people to die and go to hell because of his delay.

It was a waywardness that cost him resources that could have been used for righteousness.

It was a waywardness that indicated he did not even understand the nature of the God he had been called to serve.

Any waywardness is wrong, and you should avoid it with all your heart. But how grievous is it going to be for any of us who have to stand before God one day and answer not just for waywardness, but for great waywardness?

Chapter Three
A Study in Great Windiness

Jonah 1:4 *But the LORD sent out a great wind into the sea, and there was a mighty tempest in the sea, so that the ship was like to be broken.* **5** *Then the mariners were afraid, and cried every man unto his god, and cast forth the wares that were in the ship into the sea, to lighten it of them. But Jonah was gone down into the sides of the ship; and he lay, and was fast asleep.* **6** *So the shipmaster came to him, and said unto him, What meanest thou, O sleeper? arise, call upon thy God, if so be that God will think upon us, that we perish not.*

A divine tempest

Jonah 1:4 *But the LORD sent out a great wind into the sea, and there was a mighty tempest in the sea, so that the ship was like to be broken.*

Here is how things ended in our last chapter:

Jonah 1:3 *But Jonah rose up to flee unto Tarshish from the presence of the LORD, and went down to Joppa; and he found a ship going to Tarshish: so he paid the fare*

27

thereof, and went down into it, to go with them unto Tarshish from the presence of the LORD.

If we could encapsulate these two verses, verses three and four, here is what we would have. Verse three is Jonah exerting his will, and verse four is God exerting His will.

In verse three, Jonah determined to run from the presence of the Lord. In verse four, God informed Jonah that His presence could not be run from.

When Jonah boarded that ship, he literally thought that as the shoreline was fading from view, God was fading from view as well. He literally thought that God was somehow confined to the land of Israel.

This is a pretty important lesson to learn. The fact that God has manifested His power and presence in a special way in some special place does not mean that He is any less powerful or any less present in any other "less special" place.

God, throughout the Scripture, established borders: borders of nations, borders of towns, borders of encampments, on and on. But though God established borders, God Himself is not in the least bound by borders. He is omnipresent and needs neither a passport nor special governmental permission to be everywhere present at all times, whether we like it or not.

God, throughout Scripture, established special relationships: relationships with Abraham... Moses...David...the entire nation of Israel. But though God established special relationships, God Himself is not in the least bound by relationships. He is omnipresent and is therefore equally present among those that hate Him and those that love him, those that fear Him and those that defy Him.

God is always and everywhere God. The fact that He *takes us in* does not mean that we can *box Him in.*

Jonah was about to get quite the education on all of this.

The crew set sail, and apparently, everything started well and even went well for a while. We know that for two reasons. One, the ship would never have even set sail in some gigantic storm. They would not have even set sail if a storm was brewing. You see, even way back then they had developed excellent weather forecasting skills:

Matthew 16:1 *The Pharisees also with the Sadducees came, and tempting desired him that he would shew them a sign from heaven. **2** He answered and said unto them, When it is evening, ye say, It will be fair weather: for the sky is red. **3** And in the morning, It will be foul weather to day: for the sky is red and lowring. O ye hypocrites, ye can discern the face of the sky; but can ye not discern the signs of the times?*

Jesus acknowledged their skill at weather forecasting. And this is not the only time we find something like this in the Bible. Here is another one:

Luke 12:54 *And he said also to the people, When ye see a cloud rise out of the west, straightway ye say, There cometh a shower; and so it is. **55** And when ye see the south wind blow, ye say, There will be heat; and it cometh to pass.*

Here is another one:

Acts 27:9 *Now when much time was spent, and when sailing was now dangerous, because the fast was* *now already past, Paul admonished them,* **10** *And said unto them, Sirs, I perceive that this voyage will be with hurt and much damage, not only of the lading and ship, but also of our lives.*

This was Paul's journey to Rome. On the way there, it got late in the year. Verse nine says that the fast was already past. That was speaking of the day of atonement. That means that on our calendar, it would have been late September. Paul warned them to stay where they were for the time being; he pointed out that to sail that late in the year was dangerous.

He was right. This was commonly known among people of his day. That time of the year was the great storm season in the Mediterranean.

So the ancients knew what times of year were dangerous to sail on different bodies of water, and they knew how to forecast the weather. With the small ships they sailed in, knowing when to sail and when not to sail was literally a life or death matter.

The second way we know that it was decent weather when they left is that Jonah had gone down into the body of the ship and was asleep. A person does not casually go to sleep in the midst of a storm so bad that everyone thinks they are going to die. Jonah doubtless went to sleep when the sun was shining and the sea was calm.

These people were not dumb simpletons. So when this ship set sail, it was into what they believed was favorable weather.

Now, look at verse four again:

Jonah 1:4 *But the LORD sent out a great wind into the sea, and there was a mighty tempest in the sea, so that the ship was like to be broken.*

Who was the commonly accepted author of the book of Jonah? Jonah. And Jonah, the prophet, Jonah, the *disobedient* prophet, had an unshakable opinion as to where this great storm came from. Where did Jonah say the storm came from?

From the Lord.

This storm was so sudden, so powerful, and so deadly, everyone knew it was not just a normal thing. The Bible tells us that the ship was likely to be broken. We would not be surprised to hear of a ship being capsized by the waves or sunk by the waves, but this storm was so bad that they feared the ship would literally be shattered to pieces before it ever even sank.

This was not just a storm; it was *a divine tempest.*

A desperate attempt at survival

Jonah 1:5a *Then the mariners were afraid, and cried every man unto his god, and cast forth the wares that were in the ship into the sea, to lighten it of them...*

Like any seaport town, Joppa had people from all over the world coming and going, sailing in and sailing out. This particular crew that Jonah paid the fare to sail with were not God-fearing Israelites; they were polytheistic idolatrous heathens. Wherever they were from, they were from a people where everyone had their own individual gods.

When the divine tempest, suddenly from out of nowhere, bore down on them, these men got scared. As I have often observed, landlubbers may get easily scared about a storm out on the sea, but professional sailors and fishermen do not. They see them so often that they absolutely do not get scared easily. If a group of people like that gets scared, there is a reason to be scared.

I do not know how dedicated they were to their religion and to their "gods." Humanity being what it is, they were probably like the majority of others, meaning that their gods did not really have much of a priority in their lives.

But when this storm hit, when they realized that the ship was about to be broken to pieces, when they realized they were all about to die, they quickly got very serious about calling out to their gods! They must have reasoned that surely, between all of them, there was at least one god who could help them.

But it does not seem to have taken them long to figure out that that was not the case, because the very next thing we read is that they *"cast forth the wares that were in the ship into the sea, to lighten it of them..."*

Wares is a broad word. It is from the word kelee, and it is so broad that if we were to put it in modern vernacular, we would probably use the word "stuff." Basically, whatever they could lift, they tossed overboard; gear, tackle, freight, furniture, everything. They wanted that ship riding as high in the water as it could; they were desperate to survive and were willing to take a huge financial loss to do it.

It is amazing how facing imminent death will make people re-evaluate their priorities.

How often do we get so uptight over "stuff?" But if you knew that you were only going to live until midnight tonight, how much would that "stuff" mean to you?

They called on their gods. Their gods did not answer. So they, in a desperate attempt to survive, started throwing stuff overboard. And do you know what I find the most fascinating about all of that? The very next thing we read is that Jonah is still asleep!

A dumbfounding nap

Jonah 1:5b ...*But Jonah was gone down into the sides of the ship; and he lay, and was fast asleep.*

And he lay, and was fast asleep. A storm has crashed down on them, *and he lay, and was fast asleep.* The ship is about to be broken, *and he lay, and was fast asleep.* Everyone is screaming for their gods to save them, *and he lay, and was fast asleep.* They are throwing the furniture and freight and tackle and gear overboard, *and he lay, and was fast asleep.*

But that is not all; there are a couple more we can add. He is actively disobeying God, *and he lay, and was fast asleep.* Millions of people in Ninevah are dying and heading for hell; he has the message that can save them, *and he lay, and was fast asleep.*

This may be the most dumbfounding nap in human history. This makes Rip Van Winkle look normal.

Some years ago, I was in court for a day trying to help a family through some difficulties. There was not enough room in the courtroom for everyone who needed

33

to be there, so the judge opened up another courtroom just down the hall and sent a bunch of us over into it to wait.

Every so often, the bailiff would come in and call someone's name, and they would get up and go back into the courtroom with the judge for their trial. About halfway through the day, the bailiff came in, called out a name, and no one responded. He looked perplexed and went back into the first courtroom to see if the guy was in there. A few minutes later, he was back, calling the man's name again.

Nothing. This actually went on for a little while. Finally, he came in, said the guy's name again, and said, "This man is supposed to be in here."

About that time, someone snored very loudly...

Yep. The man who was on trial on serious charges, the man who was potentially looking at years in jail, was sound asleep. And by sound asleep, I mean that the bailiff came over and shouted at him, and he just lay there and kept snoring. He shook him, and he just lay there and kept snoring. They finally brought in smelling salts, held it under the guy's nose to wake him up!

And that man still does not hold a candle to Jonah. Jonah is about to drown, a ship full of mariners are about to die and go to hell, a city full of Ninevites are dying and going to hell, the storm is raging, people are throwing stuff overboard, people are screaming for their gods to help them, and Jonah sleeps through every bit of it.

A dramatic confrontation

Jonah 1:6 *So the shipmaster came to him, and said unto him, What meanest thou, O sleeper? arise, call upon*

34

thy God, if so be that God will think upon us, that we perish not.

As Jonah continued to sleep through it all, some of the crewmen apparently noticed, and someone told the shipmaster. That man went to where Jonah was and gave him a wake-up call. It is interesting how he started:

"What meanest thou, O sleeper?"

Let me paraphrase that for you. "Hey, you, what in the world are you doing sleeping? Does this seem like a time to sleep? Does this seem like a place to sleep? Does this seem like a situation to be sleeping in? We are all going to die very soon. I am going to die, my men are going to die, and you are going to die, so get your lazy posterior out of bed!"

The shipmaster was incredibly upset with Jonah. He wanted something from Jonah, something that Jonah had to actually be awake to do:

Jonah 1:6 *So the shipmaster came to him, and said unto him, What meanest thou, O sleeper? arise, call upon thy God, if so be that God will think upon us, that we perish not.*

Everyone else had cried out to their gods, and nothing was getting any better. So the shipmaster wanted the one guy who had not cried out to his God to get up and do so, for everyone's sake. The great windiness was so severe that this heathen was not going to leave any avenue unexplored as to how to stop it.

This really was a great windiness, it really was a divine tempest, and this lost man knew it. He had seen natural storms, plenty of them. He knew this one was something different.

Jonah was sleeping through it, though. Get that; the one guy on board who actually knew the God who caused it and the God who could stop it was the very guy who just did not care and was sleeping through it.

Christian, this world, due to its sin, is experiencing the front edge winds of a divine tempest. The storm clouds are gathering. People are going to be destroyed. And we are the ones who know the God who is bringing the storm, the God who can rescue men and women and boys and girls from it. Be awake, Christian; this world cannot afford any of God's children to be asleep.

Chapter Four
A Study in Great Wondering

Jonah 1:7 *And they said every one to his fellow, Come, and let us cast lots, that we may know for whose cause this evil is upon us. So they cast lots, and the lot fell upon Jonah.* **8** *Then said they unto him, Tell us, we pray thee, for whose cause this evil is upon us; What is thine occupation? and whence comest thou? what is thy country? and of what people art thou?* **9** *And he said unto them, I am an Hebrew; and I fear the LORD, the God of heaven, which hath made the sea and the dry land.* **10** *Then were the men exceedingly afraid, and said unto him, Why hast thou done this? For the men knew that he fled from the presence of the LORD, because he had told them.*

A desperate search for answers

Jonah 1:7 *And they said every one to his fellow, Come, and let us cast lots, that we may know for whose cause this evil is upon us. So they cast lots, and the lot fell upon Jonah.*

Let's backtrack a bit to find out just how desperate the mariners were at this point.

They had exhausted their "theological means," having prayed every man to his gods.

They had exhausted their "human means," having done everything possible to lighten the ship.

And yet still the storm raged, and still the boat was in danger of being broken apart.

It is at that point that they leaped to what just so happened to be an absolutely correct assumption:

Someone is on the ship who has made some god somewhere very, very angry.

Look at how they phrased it:

*Come, and let us cast lots, that we may know for **whose** cause this evil is upon us.*

They actually understood what "modern, enlightened man" still cannot seem to grasp; there is a God in heaven, and those disobeying Him not only put themselves at risk but others also.

Some prison missionaries I know well say that they often see the saddest of sights; a parent and a child in the same prison. The parent's choices led their children down the same worthless path.

These guys were desperate. So they "cast lots" to see who God was angry with. You see, as Matthew Henry observed, no one suspected himself, but everyone suspected someone.

The lot was sort of like drawing straws today to see who comes up with the short straw, or putting slips of paper in a bowl and pulling them out one by one and seeing who gets "the number."

Have you ever considered a couple of things? These guys were greatly wondering who the problem was, and the problem knew who he was the entire time.

How long did it take to do that which was completely unnecessary? How long did it take to prepare and cast the lots? Five minutes, ten, fifteen? However long it was, it was utterly unnecessary; Jonah could simply have spoken up.

But he did not. The one man on board who actually knew God said nothing. He gave no instructions, no directions. Pagan polytheistic heathens were left with nothing better than to use their own odd means to try and discern the mind of God.

And yet, pay attention to this, God made Himself and His mind known through the casting of those lots.

Have you ever wondered why? To me, it is not at all hard to figure out; the great God who had a great love for great sinners in Nineveh also loved those great sinners out on that boat. He had no desire that they should perish.

Pay attention to one other thing; they were not Jews. They were Gentiles. I mention that at this point because a rather well-known writer for a very famous newspaper recently tweeted a choice bit of heresy concerning the Lord Jesus and His interactions with the Syrophenician woman in Mark 7. It was the 280-character opinion of this utterly ridiculous woman that Jesus was a "repentant racist;" He "grew in His character as He wrestled with and sloughed off His formerly racist views."

Just imagine how much of that heretical drivel this witless wonder could avoid simply by procuring and reading a copy of the Old Testament book of Jonah and seeing God show such great love and compassion for Gentiles both on land and sea!

God loved these men. And so, these men in great wondering just did the best they could think of, they cast lots, and the great God of heaven answered:

So they cast lots, and the lot fell upon Jonah.

Out of everybody on the boat, it fell on Jonah. There are no coincidences with God. Ever.

A demand for specifics from Jonah

Jonah 1:8 *Then said they unto him, Tell us, we pray thee, for whose cause this evil is upon us; What is thine occupation? and whence comest thou? what is thy country? and of what people art thou?*

When the lot fell on Jonah, the mariners realized that somehow he was to blame for the storm; they just did not know how. Their first phrase, *"Tell us, we pray thee, for whose cause this evil is upon us,"* is an indication that they suspected Jonah had somehow done wrong to someone else. With a storm this bad, they likely leaped to the conclusion that he was a murderer. That is a conclusion that some others later jumped to in reference to a storm and the events that followed:

Acts 28:1 *And when they were escaped, then they knew that the island was called Melita. 2 And the barbarous people shewed us no little kindness: for they kindled a fire, and received us every one, because of the present rain, and because of the cold. 3 And when Paul had gathered a bundle of sticks, and laid them on the fire, there came a viper out of the heat, and fastened on his hand. 4 And when the barbarians saw the venomous beast* *hang on his hand, they said among themselves, No doubt this man is a murderer, whom, though he hath escaped the sea, yet vengeance suffereth not to live.*

Paul had just come through the epic storm and shipwreck of the storm Euroclydon. Then came the snake bite. They immediately assumed he was a murderer.

Whether it was that or some other great crime, the mariners reasoned that Jonah must have done something bad to someone. So, after they asked "for whose cause this evil is upon us," they immediately launched in with four more questions designed to tell them what kind of a man they were dealing with. The questions were as follows:

What is your occupation?

Where are you coming from?

What is your home country?

What is your race?

Let us take the questions one by one.

They, first of all, asked about his job. They suspected that perhaps his "line of work" is why this was happening. Maybe he was a hired killer; maybe he was a sorcerer; maybe he was a great robber.

Their second question was about where he was coming from. Was he coming from some town where he had gotten into trouble for adultery? Drunkenness? Treason?

Their third question was what his native country was. Was he of some country that especially displeased God? As Matthew Henry observes again, the Chaldaeans were well known for their divination, and the Arabians were famous for all their stealing. Was something like that the problem?

Their fourth question was what his race was. They figured his country might not tell the whole story, because countries often have different people groups within them. They wanted him to be very specific as to who he was.

A dreadful statement of facts

Jonah 1:9 *And he said unto them, I am an Hebrew; and I fear the LORD, the God of heaven, which hath made the sea and the dry land.*

How many specific questions did the mariners ask of Jonah about himself? Four.

Of those four, did Jonah answer the first, second, third, or fourth? The fourth. The very last one.

He did not answer as to his occupation. He did not answer as to where he was coming from on this trip.

He did not answer as to what country he was from.

The only thing he answered was the last question, his people, his race. You see, that was really the only thing that mattered. Not because of skin, but because of sin.

You see, Jonah was a Hebrew. And whenever the idolatrous, polytheistic nations heard that of a man, their minds immediately filled in the blanks as follows:

"A Hebrew! Oh my, their God is not at all like our gods. This is the God that was not made by man's hands. This is the God that made a covenant with man, the man Abraham, and made Himself personally known to him. This is the God that wrecked Egypt just to bring His people out of slavery. This is the God that parted the Red Sea to let His people pass over on dry ground and then collapsed those waters onto the pursuing armies of Egypt. This is not a God we want to anger!"

When Jonah told them of the God he served, it was a terrifying revelation to them. And, just in case all of that was not plain enough, he clarified it even further for them:

...and I fear the LORD, the God of heaven, which hath made the sea and the dry land.

None of the personal pagan gods could ever claim anything like this. The God Jonah was describing was utterly unique. Jonah called Him by His name: Jehovah.

This was a name that had achieved fame among the heathen for His mighty doings. Look at the words of Rahab:

Joshua 2:9 *And she said unto the men, I know that the LORD hath given you the land, and that your terror is fallen upon us, and that all the inhabitants of the land faint because of you.* **10** *For we have heard how the LORD dried up the water of the Red sea for you, when ye came out of Egypt; and what ye did unto the two kings of the Amorites, that were on the other side Jordan, Sihon and Og, whom ye utterly destroyed.*

Jehovah was different. These mariners likely had their "gods" with them right there in the boat. Their gods, the heathen gods, were small, carved out of wood, or cast out of metal. They went somewhere and bought these "gods" and carried them around with them.

Now put yourself in the place of one of those pagan mariners, carrying your god around, your god that is about to sink to the bottom of the sea along with you, and you hear Jonah say these words:

...and I fear the LORD, the God of heaven, which hath made the sea and the dry land.

Jonah's God was not going to sink into the sea; His God made the sea and the dry land. This was a very different God that these men were now dealing with, and they knew it.

But they knew something else, too. And the something else they knew came from a bit of information they got before they ever left the dock:

Jonah 1:10 *Then were the men exceedingly afraid, and said unto him, Why hast thou done this?* ***For the men knew that he fled from the presence of the LORD, because he had told them.***

Commentator Matthew Poole said, "He had told them, when they inquired the cause of his travels, as it is very like they would do, ***ere they took his fare.***" (Poole)

In other words, just as the words in verse ten clearly imply, Jonah told them he was running from God when he first got on the boat. It is very doubtful that he told them *which* God he was running from, since they were not scared before, but they knew he was running from his God.

In other words, at some point before leaving the shore, a conversation something like this seems to have taken place:

Jonah: Hello, um, I would like to purchase a ticket to sail today. Whom do I need to speak to about that?

Mariner: You can talk to me, I sail and work for one of the finest shipping companies to sail the Great Sea. Where is it exactly you want to go?

Jonah: Well, if possible, I would like to go to Tarshish.

Mariner: (laughing) Tarshish? What makes a man want to sail all the way to the end of the earth? Surely the little woman can't be that bad!

Jonah: No, no, nothing like that. I am actually sailing for, well, a "religious reason."

Mariner: Religion? No offense intended, buddy, but there are more "gods" in these parts than you can shake a stick at. If you can't find a god to serve here, what makes you think you can find one all the way out in Tarshish?

Jonah: Well, actually, I have the opposite problem. I already have a God. I am not trying to find a God; I am trying to get away from the one I do have!

Mariner: (laughing uproariously) Now in all my years of sailing, that one is a first for me. But the good news is, you're in luck. We just so happen to have a ship sailing out for Tarshish in one hour. Leave your god lying around somewhere in here and be on board in half an hour. And don't worry, someone will no doubt pick your god up and take it home and take very good care of it. Leave your god and your troubles here, friend. Next stop: Tarshish.

But once the storm hit, and once they pressed Jonah further, oh, how very different they found out that Jonah's God was from their gods!

But how sad, how very sad they had to find out the way that they did. How sad that they did not find it out instead from the lips of a soul-winning prophet, rather than from the chastisement of a disobedient prophet.

Our God is different, so very different than the "gods" that this world has to offer. And they will find out at some point, one way or another. May it never be said of us that they found out by observing and even getting inadvertently caught up in the chastisement He brings upon us rather than by hearing it from us out of concern for their souls.

Chapter Five
A Study in Great Wretchedness

Jonah 1:11 *Then said they unto him, What shall we do unto thee, that the sea may be calm unto us? for the sea wrought, and was tempestuous. 12 And he said unto them, Take me up, and cast me forth into the sea; so shall the sea be calm unto you: for I know that for my sake this great tempest is upon you. 13 Nevertheless the men rowed hard to bring it to the land; but they could not: for the sea wrought, and was tempestuous against them. 14 Wherefore they cried unto the LORD, and said, We beseech thee, O LORD, we beseech thee, let us not perish for this man's life, and lay not upon us innocent blood: for thou, O LORD, hast done as it pleased thee. 15 So they took up Jonah, and cast him forth into the sea: and the sea ceased from her raging. 16 Then the men feared the LORD exceedingly, and offered a sacrifice unto the LORD, and made vows.*

A desperate question

Jonah 1:11 *Then said they unto him, What shall we do unto thee, that the sea may be calm unto us? for the sea wrought, and was tempestuous.*

Let's begin with the last part of this verse first, since it gives the cause of their question in the first part of the verse.

The Bible could have just said that the sea was tempestuous, that would have been enough to convey that the storm was really bad. But God specifically chose to say that the sea *"wrought, and was tempestuous."*

The word tempestuous means that it was raging. That sounds fairly normal for a bad storm. But the word wrought is from a Hebrew word that most commonly means to walk. That is not normal at all! In fact, it is so abnormal that in all of the storms found in Scripture, this is the only one of them ever described with that word.

I doubt very seriously if any of us have ever described the sea as "walking." But you see, all any of us have ever likely seen are natural storms. Natural storms operate in destructive but largely regular ways. This storm was a supernatural storm. As these mariners looked out on it, all of their experience on the sea told them that this was not being caused by nature but by something or someone supernatural. The sea seemed as if it were "walking." Picture being out on the ocean in a gigantic storm, and it looking very much like the waves are taking huge steps and trying to stomp you to the bottom of the ocean floor. That is basically what the text means when it says that the sea wrought and was tempestuous.

These men were scared, these men were in trouble, and they knew that Jonah was the source of their trouble. And yet pay attention to the fact that they asked Jonah what they should do with him! Rather than just jumping to a conclusion, they actually asked Jonah for his counsel.

This was amazingly wise on their part. They had already determined that the God of Jonah had sent this storm. They had already evaluated Jonah's God against their gods and come to the conclusion that their gods were pitiful and powerless against Jonah's God. The last thing in the world they wanted was to offend the very God who was sending that storm!

So, since they did not have a relationship with Jonah's God, and Jonah—despite his backslidden condition did—they asked Jonah what they should do.

If you are in the middle of a storm and that storm has been caused by a disobedient stranger in your midst, and you have to turn to that disobedient stranger to ask him what should be done, that truly is a desperate question!

A deceptive answer

Jonah 1:12 *And he said unto them, Take me up, and cast me forth into the sea; so shall the sea be calm unto you: for I know that for my sake this great tempest is upon you.*

There is much in Jonah's answer that is a lot like the sea itself; you have to look below the surface to find out what is in it.

On the surface, Jonah's answer seems almost heart-touching:

"Forsooth! Tis for my wretchedness that all of you men now tremble and fear for your lives. It is I, Jonah, and I alone that must needs be sacrificed. I dare not, nay I CANNOT countenance the unthinkable notion that you should perish along with me.

Take me up at once! Cast me into the raging depths of the sea! I will sacrifice myself that all of you might then live. Go home to your families, raise your children, and when you look upon their smiling faces, do me the honor of remembering me, the man who gave his own life that yours may be spared..."

But that is simply not the case. This was, in fact, a deceptive answer. You see, there are two ways an answer can be deceptive; in its message or in its motive. Jonah's message was verifiably right. He told them that if they cast him into the sea, everything would calm down. They cast him into the sea; everything calmed down.

But the motive? That is another story entirely.

What is it, very specifically, that God had commanded Jonah to do? Go to Nineveh and preach. May I make a very profound, deep, scientific statement that perhaps no one has ever made before?

Dead men don't preach. (Yes, yes, I know, you are quite sure you have actually had to sit through messages so boring and dry that it must have been dead men preaching them...)

What it boils down to is that Jonah would literally rather die than obey. If Jonah's motive had been right, his answer would have been different. You see, all Jonah would have had to do to get the sea to calm down was say the words, "turn the boat around, take me back to shore." But again, Jonah would literally rather die than obey.

And I suppose that in many cases God would allow that. But you see, God had raised Jonah up and given Jonah the ability to preach powerfully and convincingly, and He had done so because a couple of million people in Nineveh needed it! So God was not going to let Jonah take those God-given gifts to a watery grave along with his disobedient self.

How wretched was Jonah to be willing, even desirous of drowning rather than to take the Gentiles the gospel.

A dramatic effort

Jonah 1:13 *Nevertheless the men rowed hard to bring it to the land; but they could not: for the sea wrought, and was tempestuous against them.*

The men had asked what to do, and Jonah had answered.

These men are now given a way out. Jonah says, "Throw me overboard, and the sea will stop raging, and you will all live." You may think differently, but I really appreciate what I read next:

Jonah 1:13 *Nevertheless the men rowed hard to bring it to the land; but they could not: for the sea wrought, and was tempestuous against them.*

These men, unlike a lot of people today, had a high regard for the sanctity of life! These men put their backs and biceps to the oars and rowed like mad-men trying to get the boat to land just to save one wretched life.

51

Oh, how I wish some "modern, enlightened" people held that same high view of life, starting with innocent babes in the womb!

The mariners tried, they gave their best effort, but at last, realized they were beaten.

Jonah 1:14 *Wherefore they cried unto the LORD, and said, We beseech thee, O LORD, we beseech thee, let us not perish for this man's life, and lay not upon us innocent blood: for thou, O LORD, hast done as it pleased thee.* **15** *So they took up Jonah, and cast him forth into the sea: and the sea ceased from her raging.*

Earlier in the chapter, in verse five, each of these men were crying out to their own personal little gods, and pay attention; it did not help. This is yet one more excellent proof of the fact that not all beliefs are equally valid. The growing popularity of relativism in our day tells me that people ignore the fact that not all beliefs are valid and ignore logic along the way to arrive at their desired conclusion.

Some years ago, I wrote the following newspaper column wondering aloud what would happen if the tenets of relativism were put to the test.

"The World Conference Of Relativism"

John 8:32, "And ye shall know the truth, and the truth shall make you free."

As a Bible-believing Christian, I not only believe that it is absolutely true, but I also believe that there is such a thing as absolute truth. But I am mindful of the fact that, in our day, some people no longer believe that there even is such a thing as absolute truth...

Unbeknownst to most, the World Conference of Relativism was recently held in a top-secret location. Thanks to my world-class inside sources, though, I have been given a firsthand recounting of all of the fun that took place.

As the masses arrived in the large open field, there were smiles all around to begin the day. A platform could be seen in the distance with a podium for the lofty exalted authorities of the doctrine of relativism to speak from. Banners adorned the stage bearing messages that said, "Live your own truth," "All Truth Is Relative," "All Beliefs Are Equally Valid," and "There Is No Absolute Truth."

Jumbotrons and speakers would make sure that everyone could see and hear the wisdom that would doubtless be pouring forth.

It did not take long, though, for the problems to begin.

As a group of people from Georgia arrived, they began to push their way through the crowd to get as near to the front as they could. That did not sit very well with a group from Boston who got very upset with what they immediately perceived as white privilege.

"Well, if that isn't typical! A bunch of privileged whites thinking they own the world and can go to the front of whatever line there happens to be," one of the men from Boston said snarkily. The crowd from Georgia, though, took great umbrage with that characterization.

"I will have you know, sir", replied one of the ladies from Georgia, "that all of us are black. It may not look like it to you, but that is how each and every one of us identifies, and we are just living out our truth."

"Sir!" The man from Boston snapped, "did you just call me 'sir?'" How dare you assume such a thing based solely on my anatomy, long beard, and deep bass voice!"

As the argument escalated, other groups moved to intervene, and that only served to worsen the entire brawl. A group of people there to protest fat-shaming were accosted by another group wanting to battle epidemic obesity. In turn, the epidemic obesity crowd began to be pelted with boos from an advocacy group wanting to let everyone know that starvation in our country is running rampant.

A woman's rights contingent ran into even greater problems. They were railed on by proponents of Sharia law and told that they should not be seen in public without a male family member. Some were even beaten. When the women began to protest, they were met with shouts of "Islamophobia!"

"Stop! Stop!" a voice suddenly boomed over the loudspeakers. "We will have no violence or hatred in this place! All of your beliefs are equally valid, and we are here for something too important for any of us to be distracted from. What is our theme for this meeting? 'There is no such thing as absolute truth.' Everyone must be free to live out their own truth, right?"

"And who are you to judge?" a voice from the crowd shouted back. "How dare you accuse us of violence or hatred!"

"But, but, you people are hitting each other, cursing and swearing at each other, and pulling each other's hair!" the voice over the speaker retorted.

"Says who?" the voice from the crowd shot back. "I say we have all been perfectly peaceful. That is my truth, and I have every right to it."

There was a moment of silence, then the voice from the loudspeaker spoke one last time. "Yes, I suppose you are correct, as am I, and as is everyone else here, depending upon their perspective. By all means, carry on with your own individual truth. I am going to cash my speaker's check and go home. After all, wisdom like mine is worth every penny of it."

Had the mariners of Jonah's day been in attendance, they would have pleaded with everyone never to be so foolish as to think that all beliefs, or all gods, are equally valid. These men cried out to their gods, and none of them helped or could help.

But now, after having experienced the storm and after rowing hard to bring it to land and finding out that they could not, they cry out to the LORD, all capital letters, Jehovah, the God of Jonah, three times. This was the right thing to do and the right God to call out to. Hallelujah, they finally got to that point!

But how sad is it that they did so in spite of Jonah, not because of Jonah. Jonah was so wretched at this point that he gave them no really good witness at all. Again, he was behaving like a man who would rather die than obey.

This truly was great wretchedness on the part of Jonah. He was not only putting his own life at risk but the lives and eternal souls of the mariners and of the millions of men, women, and children in Nineveh. He would rather die than obey, because to obey would mean to take God's message to people that, in his view, did not deserve it.

There is a good way to keep this from ever being the way we think and behave. Just decide now to take the gospel always and only to people who *do not* deserve it. You see, since no one deserves it, including us, that will spare us any confusion whatsoever in whom we ought to be reaching.

Chapter Six
A Study in Great Wisdom

Jonah 1:17 *Now the LORD had prepared a great fish to swallow up Jonah. And Jonah was in the belly of the fish three days and three nights.*

The wisdom of preparation

Jonah 1:17a *Now the LORD had prepared a great fish to swallow up Jonah.*

We arrive now at the controversial/not at all controversial portion of the book of Jonah. I say it that way because, in truth, it is only controversial to people who do not believe in God and therefore do not believe in the miraculous.

If the verse had said, "Now, a great fish swallowed up Jonah," please let me tell you what we would be left with and what conclusion an honest person would arrive at. If that is what the text said, we would be left with the question as to whether or not any great fish, or a whale as Matthew 12:40 says, could swallow a man whole. And what we would find is that, at least in theory, yes, there are. There are actually multiple fish/whales that would qualify.

By the way, do not get sidetracked by people telling you that a whale is not a fish. Those taxonomic classifications are ours, not God's. If the God who created every creature wants to regard this very special whale as a fish, He has every right and authority to do so.

It is at this point that you likely expect me to list the sea creatures that could potentially have swallowed Jonah whole. And there would be nothing at all wrong with that, and I have no quarrel at all with those who do.

But I am not going to do so for one very simple reason: it is utterly unnecessary. Look at the text again, and let me show you the word that makes it utterly unnecessary:

Jonah 1:17a *Now the LORD had **prepared** a great fish to swallow up Jonah.*

God saw to it that there would be a fish capable of swallowing a man; He prepared this. God saw to it that the fish would swallow the man; He prepared this. This word means to ordain something, but it does not, as many commentaries say, simply mean that He took an already, naturally existing fish and appointed it to be in place.

They say that because of the Hebrew word that the English word "prepared" comes from, which is the word *mawnaw*. Oftentimes it does mean simply to ordain, to set in place.

But let me show you something very interesting. The word "prepared" occurs seventy-six times in the Old Testament. Out of those seventy-six times, only four times does it come from that Hebrew word *mawnaw*.

You already know that one of them is right here in Jonah 1:17. Let me show you the only other three times in the Old Testament that it comes from that particular word, and you see what very obvious thing there is to notice:

Jonah 4:6 *And the LORD God **prepared** a gourd, and made it to come up over Jonah, that it might be a shadow over his head, to deliver him from his grief. So Jonah was exceeding glad of the gourd.*

Jonah 4:7 *But God **prepared** a worm when the morning rose the next day, and it smote the gourd that it withered.*

Jonah 4:8 *And it came to pass, when the sun did arise, that God **prepared** a vehement east wind; and the sun beat upon the head of Jonah, that he fainted, and wished in himself to die, and said, It is better for me to die than to live.*

What do you happen to notice about the only four times in the entire Old Testament that the word prepared comes from that word *mawnaw*? All of them are right here in the book of Jonah.

And what do you notice about the four things God prepared? God prepared a fish, and it was so unnatural that not only was it able to swallow a man, it was able to keep him alive in its stomach for three days and nights and then regurgitate him on demand. God prepared a gourd that was so unnatural that it sprang up in a single night to such a considerable size that it was able to overshadow a man, and it did so right on the spot where a man was sitting that needed to be overshadowed. God prepared a worm that was so unnatural that it was able to destroy that gourd in just a day. God prepared an east wind so unnatural that it beat down on Jonah and made him want to die, and it started blowing at just the right time after the gourd was destroyed.

What I am saying is, this word prepared means much more than God simply picking out a specific fish that was already suitable for the job. In the context of these four usages of the word "prepared" in the book of Jonah, it clearly means that He specifically designed and created that fish for this unique purpose.

The God of all power and sovereignty did not wring His hands and wish for a fish, nor did He search through the sea for a fish; He had a fish prepared and ready to go. This whole affair was not natural; it was supernatural. Had God chosen to do so, He could have prepared a clam to swallow Jonah. God does not answer to nature; nature answers to God.

But think of the incredible foresight this took! The gourd and worm and wind were immediate products. The text tells us that they happened all at once; it says that God prepared them, and they were there. But it does not say that about the fish; when speaking of the fish in Jonah 1:17, it says that God *had* prepared a fish. It was not instantly made when needed like the gourd and worm and wind; it was done ahead of time.

How long must all of that have taken? How many years was it growing? It does not say He "Poof! Spoke it into existence;" it says He "had prepared" it.

In other words, God was ready for Jonah's sin before Jonah ever even thought of sinning. God knew Jonah would run before Jonah ever ran. God knew how big Jonah would be when he ran and how big of a fish it would take to swallow him.

While Jonah was young and happy-go-lucky, God in His foresight had a great fish growing and being specifically designed out in the Mediterranean.

While Jonah was living the life of a land-lubber, God in His foresight had a great fish growing and being specifically designed out in the Mediterranean.

When Jonah first got the call to preach and was on fire to serve God, God, in His foresight, had a great fish growing and being specifically designed out in the Mediterranean.

When Jonah was told to go to Nineveh, hundreds of miles inland, God in His foresight had a great fish growing and being specifically designed out in the Mediterranean.

Let this sink in; God wants you to do right. But even if you do wrong, He is still God, and He is not thrown off track. If you do right for years and years and years and then suddenly turn on a dime and do wrong, you are going to find out that the entire time you were doing right, the God of heaven in His wisdom and foresight was already preparing to deal with your wrong the entire time you were doing right!

The wisdom of placement

Jonah 1:17a *Now the LORD had prepared a great fish to swallow up Jonah.*

Please allow me to ask you some questions. One: in what body of water was that fish? The Mediterranean sea. Two: on what body of water was Jonah? The Mediterranean sea.

Good; you know the answers to the first two questions. But now I have a third question: how big is the Mediterranean sea?

That one you most likely do not know the answer to, so allow me to fill in the details for you. The answer is 965,300 square miles. To simplify that, we can legitimately say that it is almost a million square miles.

Please think of an adjective to describe a million square miles; how would you describe that much area? Massive? Monstrous? Huge? Yes to all of that.

But wait, there's more...

The Mediterranean Sea has an average depth of nearly a mile, and in places like the Calypso Deep, it is more than three miles deep. All of that means that there are approximately 147 *quadrillion* cubic feet of water in the Mediterranean sea!

Now here is another question. How long can a man likely survive when thrown out of a boat out in the open ocean in the midst of a storm worse than any other storm has ever been, a storm so bad that seasoned mariners recognized it as literally a supernatural storm?

A few seconds. Certainly well under a minute.

Are you putting all of the math together in your minds yet? Out of 147 quadrillion cubic feet of water, out of a million square miles, out of a depth as shallow as the very surface of the water all the way down to 3 miles, in a raging, blinding storm, if Jonah was going to have any chance at all to survive, that fish had to literally be right there in the exact spot where and when he was thrown overboard.

And he was. There was absolutely nothing "natural" about any of this. This was the God of all wisdom showing His wisdom by the utterly perfect placement of that fish. The odds on that one fish accidentally being in just the right place at just the right time is, to put it bluntly, impossible.

What did we say the book of Jonah is? A study in greatness. In light of the wisdom of His placement, how great is our God!

The wisdom of purpose

Jonah 1:17 *Now the LORD had prepared a great fish to swallow up Jonah. And Jonah was in the belly of the fish three days and three nights.*

To demonstrate what I have in mind as we begin to deal with this point, please allow me to ask you yet another question. Since God clearly wanted to keep Jonah alive when he was thrown overboard, and since God is clearly a miraculous God, how many potential ways were there that God could have used to save Jonah?

Infinite.

He could have, for instance, used something like what He used with Elijah when He took him to heaven:

2 Kings 2:11 *And it came to pass, as they still went on, and talked, that, behold, there appeared a chariot of fire, and horses of fire, and parted them both asunder; and Elijah went up by a whirlwind into heaven.*

Had God so chosen, we could have ended up reading something similar in Jonah 1:17:

65

"Now the Lord had prepared a whirlwind and a chariot of fire and horses of fire, and God caught up Jonah as he was cast overboard, and carried him away to safety."

God was not limited to a fish; He chose a fish.

Had God so chosen, He could have used a cloud, just as Jesus did during His ascension:

Acts 1:9 *And when he had spoken these things, while they beheld, he was taken up; and a cloud received him out of their sight.*

So in Jonah 1:17, we could have actually ended up reading, "And as they tossed him overboard, he was taken up; and a cloud received him out of their sight."

It very literally could have been anything.

"And God prepared a great seagull, who caught Jonah up and took him to safety."

"And God prepared a great dolphin, who swam up under Jonah, and carried him gayly through the waves back to shore."

"And God prepared a great iceberg, one that would not melt in the warm waters of the Mediterranean, and Jonah landed upon it, and thus it floated to shore with him."

With an omnipotent God, all of this, any of this, and infinitely more was possible. In other words, God chose to save Jonah by a fish for a very specific purpose or purposes.

May I offer two very obvious ones?

One, this gave Jonah three days in the belly of that fish to get good and miserable and realize that he was in a horrible predicament because of his own stubbornness and rebellion.

How often is that the case with us? How often do we very "Jonah-like" people even today get ourselves into the worst of predicaments because of our own stubbornness and rebellion?

Some years ago, there was a young man in our church who, to put it bluntly, was the most stubborn human being I had ever met. If I preached something, he did the exact opposite. If his parents said something, he did the exact opposite. Naturally, all of the things we warned him would eventually happen started happening. And so it was that he found himself in the hospital as a direct result of his own choices.

I went to visit him. It is what pastors do, even if they are so frustrated that they want to simply stay home and send a text that simply says, "I told you so."

When I walked into the room, the whining began.

"Preacher! Why is this happening? Why is God being so hard on me?"

Without so much as a second of hesitation, I replied, "Because you're stupid."

His eyes got as big as yours probably got when you read that. But I was not done yet.

"Everything I have ever preached, you have ignored and done the exact opposite, even though it was all straight from the Word of God. Everything your parents have ever said you have ignored and done the exact opposite, even though it was all straight from the Word of God. You are stubborn and rebellious, and you are getting exactly what you deserve."

There is really no need to rub salve on someone who can only benefit from a needed kick in the posterior.

Jonah did not need salve; he needed three days in a fish's belly to realize how stupid and stubborn and rebellious he had been.

Two, this time in the belly of the fish gave Jonah something very unexpected and special in regards to his eventual preaching in Nineveh.

The Ninevites had multiple deities that they worshiped. A particular one that archaeologists have discovered in the ruins of Nineveh was called Dagon. Dagon, ladies and gentlemen, was "the fish god." He was a man from the waist up and a fish from the waist down.

Not to get too far ahead of things, but when Jonah walked into Nineveh to preach, he did so having spent three days and nights in the stomach acids of a great fish and having lived to tell about it. A story like this travels fast. Jonah would have been a walking wonder to everyone in Nineveh. God used even the rebellion of Jonah to accomplish his purposes for Nineveh. I am not even beginning to imply that we ever *should* rebel; I am saying that our God is of such great wisdom that He can even turn our rebellion into something useful.

The wisdom of prophecy

Jonah 1:17b *And Jonah was in the belly of the fish three days and three nights.*

Throughout the Old Testament, God never, not even for a moment, took His eyes off of the ultimate goal. Revelation 13:8 calls Jesus "the Lamb slain from the foundation of the world."

The death, burial, and resurrection of Christ is what all of the Old Testament Scripture pointed to; it is what all of the Old Testament was about.

When Abraham was walking up the mountain thinking of the anguish of having to offer up his son, Isaac, God was thinking of His Son, who would one day be slain on that very mountain.

When the Children of Israel were sprinkling the blood of a lamb on the doorposts there in Egypt so the destroyer would pass over them, God was thinking about His Son who would shed His blood for others on an old rugged cross.

And when Jonah was spending three days and three nights in that fish's belly, let me show you what God was thinking:

Matthew 12:39 *But he answered and said unto them, An evil and adulterous generation seeketh after a sign; and there shall no sign be given to it, but the sign of the prophet Jonas:* **40** *For as Jonas was three days and three nights in the whale's belly; so shall the Son of man be three days and three nights in the heart of the earth.*

Jonah thought he was running from the presence of God when he got on that boat. Jonah thought he was thwarting God when he had the mariners throw him overboard. But the entire time, the all-wise God of heaven was saying, "When Jonah goes overboard, that will be a great opportunity for me to use a fish as a prophecy of the fact that my Son will spend three days and three nights laying in the ground."

That is some incomparable wisdom!

What is the book of Jonah? A study in greatness. And when it comes to wisdom, there is absolutely none so great as our God.

Chapter Seven
A Study in Great Will Breaking

Jonah 2:1 *Then Jonah prayed unto the LORD his God out of the fish's belly,* **2** *And said, I cried by reason of mine affliction unto the LORD, and he heard me; out of the belly of hell cried I, and thou heardest my voice.* **3** *For thou hadst cast me into the deep, in the midst of the seas; and the floods compassed me about: all thy billows and thy waves passed over me.* **4** *Then I said, I am cast out of thy sight; yet I will look again toward thy holy temple.* **5** *The waters compassed me about, even to the soul: the depth closed me round about, the weeds were wrapped about my head.* **6** *I went down to the bottoms of the mountains; the earth with her bars was about me for ever: yet hast thou brought up my life from corruption, O LORD my God.* **7** *When my soul fainted within me I remembered the LORD: and my prayer came in unto thee, into thine holy temple.* **8** *They that observe lying vanities forsake their own mercy.* **9** *But I will sacrifice unto thee with the voice of thanksgiving; I will pay that that I have vowed. Salvation is of the LORD.* **10** *And the LORD spake unto the fish, and it vomited out Jonah upon the dry land.*

A matter of timing

Jonah 2:1 ***Then*** *Jonah prayed unto the LORD his God out of the fish's belly,*

The little four-letter word "then" that starts Jonah 2 is, to me, one of the most stunning words in Scripture when used here. It gives us a matter of timing when we compare it to the last verse of chapter one. To show you what I mean about it being stunning, let's read words of the last verse of chapter one and the first verse of chapter two back to back:

"*Now the LORD had prepared a great fish to swallow up Jonah. And Jonah was in the belly of the fish three days and three nights.* ***Then*** *Jonah prayed unto the LORD his God out of the fish's belly.*"

Then. After three days and three nights in the stomach of a fish. Ask yourself something, if you were in the stomach of a fish and you knew that you were there because of your sinfulness, how long would it take you to start praying?

For Jonah, the answer was three days and three nights!

I think you will be hard-pressed to find anyone anywhere either in the pages of Scripture or even in your own personal experience, with all of the people you have met, with any more of a stubborn will than Jonah.

Just for a moment, place yourself in the mind of Jonah there in the belly of that fish. Let me tell you the facts that would be bouncing around in your brain.

One: God told me to go to Nineveh, and I refused to do so. Two: I tried to run from God by getting on a boat for Tarshish, and yet God did not let me get away with it.

He caused a great storm in the ocean designed to get me to get the sailors to turn the boat around and go to shore. Three: rather than have them turn the boat around, I had them throw me overboard, hoping I could drown and die without having to go to Nineveh. Four: God had a great fish very carefully swallow me. It could have been a shark that ripped me to pieces, but instead, it was a fish that simply swallowed me. I am still alive. I am able to breathe in this foul stench of a fish's belly. Five: a God this powerful is therefore clearly powerful enough to pick me up and carry me to Nineveh and to drop me right in the midst of them. Does He still want me to go? Yes, otherwise I would not still be alive. But since He has not just carried me there and dropped me in the midst of them, He wants me to submit to His will and go there in submission to Him, not forced by Him.

Conclusion: all I have to do is bow my will to His, and this can all be over. He will get me out of this fish's belly once I humble myself before Him.

Those are all of the facts that, if you were Jonah, would be bouncing around in your brain. And all of that is what makes the word "then" so very stunning. Knowing all of this, knowing that all he had to do to get out of his predicament was finally submit himself to God, he stubbornly held out for seventy-two hours inside of that fish's belly.

But may I submit to you that even seeing it as seventy-two hours does not quite do it justice? What I mean by that is that while he was there in the fish's belly, he obviously did not have access to sunlight or a watch or a calendar. By the time the words of the book of Jonah were put to paper, God had let him know that it was seventy-two hours, all Scripture is given by inspiration of God. But while he was there in the fish's belly, he was there in the dark for seventy-two hours, and it had to feel like weeks, I would imagine.

Prisoners in concentration camps often scratched marks on the wall to keep track of how many days they had been there. It gave them some sense of sanity, some sense of perspective. They could see the sun set and rise, and they knew how many days were passing.

Jonah, in his absolute hardhearted rebellion and stubbornness, was in the belly of that fish in the darkness for seventy-two hours that had to feel like weeks. He was willing to endure the stench and the darkness and the constantly being wet and the stomach acids eating at his skin for three days and three nights.

But finally, we come to that wonderful word "then" when Jonah's stubborn will finally broke.

A matter of turning

Jonah 2:2 *And said, I cried by reason of mine affliction unto the LORD, and he heard me; out of the belly of hell cried I, and thou heardest my voice.*

From this verse until the next to last verse of this chapter, Jonah is recounting the prayer that he prayed. What makes it very interesting as you read it is that it seems much more a prayer of deliverance than of desperation. In other words, Jonah, in this prayer, speaks of his deliverance as if it had already happened before it actually happened. Jonah is praying in repentance, yes, but he is also praying in faith. Once his stubbornness finally was jettisoned, his confidence in God began to soar.

As verse two begins, Jonah says, *"I cried by reason of mine affliction unto the LORD."*

It was affliction, in this case, in the form of the chastening hand of God, that broke Jonah's stubborn will and got him praying in earnest. Jonah was like many stubborn people today; they cry out to the Lord because of their affliction, not because of their affection. People's lives would be so much better off if they would have enough affection for God to obey Him immediately and not have to undergo the affliction of chastisement from God.

It did not have to be that way. Jonah could have prayed back home in Gathhepher of Galilee. Jonah could have prayed on the way to Nineveh. But Jonah is having to pray out of the belly of the fish because of his disobedience. And it is the affliction that he underwent as chastisement for his disobedience that finally made him cry out to the Lord.

I wish that this were an exceedingly uncommon thing, but it is not. As of the writing of this book, I have been alive for forty-nine years and a pastor for twenty-one years, and I can tell you this is incredibly common. People push God away and neglect His Word and do not pray and live however they want to live and rebel against the commandments of God and the will of God, and there finally comes a point at which God lowers the hammer on them and blows their world to pieces and then, then, then they finally cry out to the Lord.

Jonah specifically said he cried out to the Lord because of his affliction.

The next phrase he uttered, though, has caused some interesting moments through the years. Jonah said, *"out of the belly of hell cried I."*

A great many times through the years, I have heard preachers proclaim, based on this phrase, that Jonah died in the belly of that fish and actually spent three days in hell. That is absolutely not the case.

Our generation was not the first one to come up with the idea of speaking metaphorically. Scripture itself is loaded with people using metaphorical speech. Here is an example of that again concerning hell:

Psalm 139:8 *If I ascend up into heaven, thou art there:* ***if I make my bed in hell***, *behold, thou art there.*

Are there really beds in hell? Maybe Sleep Number beds with organic cotton sheets and My Pillow pillow toppers? No. The psalmist was speaking metaphorically to convey a literal truth.

When Jonah said that he cried unto the Lord out of the belly of hell, he was using the exact same type of speech we use when we describe something as being "hell on earth." This is not at all hard to figure out when you read the rest of this chapter. Everything that Jonah describes in this chapter is about being in the belly of the fish in the depths of the sea. Nothing that Jonah describes in this chapter is about being in hell.

Would being in the belly of the fish be a horrible thing? Certainly. But compared to being in hell, would being in the belly of a fish be a horrible thing? No! Compared to being in hell, being in the belly of the fish would be a trip to Disney World. And yet we are told by some to believe that Jonah went into the belly of the fish, then died and went to hell, then was resurrected there in the belly of that fish, and then when he wrote about it later had no details and no complaints about hell whatsoever and had only details and complaints about being in the fish's belly.

Jonah did not die and go to hell. But the belly of the fish was awful enough to him that he described it by saying, "*out of the belly of hell cried I.*"

But the last part of verse two is the crowning jewel: "*...and thou heardest my voice.*"

Jonah found out that the God who was aware of his rebellion and aware of his stubbornness was also aware of his repentance and was instantly willing to hear and answer when he cried out for help.

God is so much more merciful than we are and so much quicker to mercy than we are. Rebellious Jonah cried out to God, and the holy God of heaven instantly heard him.

Jonah 2:3 *For thou hadst cast me into the deep, in the midst of the seas; and the floods compassed me about: all thy billows and thy waves passed over me.*

As Jonah continued praying, he gave us something interesting in the grammar of verse three that often goes overlooked. We can see clearly from this verse what I said a moment ago about Jonah being in the water, not in hell. The five words he used it to describe it here were deep, seas, floods, billows, and waves. There is no doubt whatsoever that Jonah was describing literally being in the belly of the fish, in the water. But what is interesting in the grammar of verse three is a small change that Jonah makes from the first two sections of the verse to the last section of the verse. Take a look at it and see if you can figure out what it is.

He changes from the word "the" to the word "thy."

Look at it again:

Jonah 2:3 *For thou hadst cast me into **the** deep, in the midst of **the** seas; and **the** floods compassed me about: all **thy** billows and **thy** waves passed over me.*

Jonah is praying, and he is mentioning all that he is going through, but it seems to have dawned on his heart as he spoke that he was missing the personal aspect of it. All of this that he was going through was not just a "the" thing; it was a "thy" thing. God made the deep and the seas and the floods and the billows and the waves, and He was using everything that He had made and that He had ownership and possession of and a right over to break the stubborn will of His servant whom He had also made and over whom He also had ownership and possession of and a right over.

Jonah 2:4 *Then I said, I am cast out of thy sight; yet I will look again toward thy holy temple.*

There is something in verse four that is both remarkable and poignant, and that ties into an earlier part of the text. Look back at Jonah 1:3, please.

Jonah 1:3 *But Jonah rose up to flee unto Tarshish **from the presence of the LORD**, and went down to Joppa; and he found a ship going to Tarshish: so he paid the fare thereof, and went down into it, to go with them unto Tarshish **from the presence of the LORD**.*

As the story began, Jonah was trying desperately to get away from God, to get away from His presence. He did not want God seeing him. But once he got into a place where he felt like God actually was not looking his way anymore, desperation and heartbreak broke over Jonah.

Jonah got what he wanted and found out that it was the last thing he needed.

Jonahs are everywhere. There are Jonahs on the job and Jonahs at school and Jonahs in our families and Jonahs in the church choir and Jonahs on the pews and Jonahs in the pulpit. Everywhere you go, there are people who, in practice, are trying to get out of God's sight and away from His gaze, only to find out that the most miserable existence on earth is to feel like God is not looking your way anymore.

As soon as Jonah felt like God was looking his way, he said, "I will look again toward thy holy temple." Whether he had the Temple of Jerusalem in mind or the Temple of God in heaven, Jonah wanted to get a glimpse of God again, hoping to see God looking his way once more.

Jonah 2:5 *The waters compassed me about, even to the soul: the depth closed me round about, the weeds were wrapped about my head.*

Jonah speaks both emotionally and literally in this verse. He talks about the waters compassing him about, closing in on him, and he says it was even to his soul. Jonah was getting claustrophobic in every possible way; physically, emotionally, and spiritually.

And one thing that was very literally happening during all of that is the weeds were wrapped around his head. This creature was ingesting seaweed, slurping it down into his stomach, and that nasty stuff was wrapping around Jonah's head and getting him tangled up in it.

Jonah 2:6 *I went down to the bottoms of the mountains; the earth with her bars was about me for ever: yet hast thou brought up my life from corruption, O LORD my God.*

Once again, in this verse, Jonah speaks both emotionally and literally. Showing an excellent understanding of geographical truths, thousands of years before it was ever able to be verified by modern technology, Jonah spoke of going down to the bottoms of the mountains. People did not always understand that many of the mountains have as much or more to them under the water as they do on the land.

This fish took Jonah way down deep into the sea. Even in the relative protection of the fish's belly, the pressure on Jonah had to be incredible. I can only imagine the earaches and the migraines that he was enduring.

He said, *"the earth with her bars was about me for ever:"* he was speaking metaphorically again, picturing himself as a prisoner for whom there was no escape and no hope. But then he ended verse six this way:

"Yet hast thou brought up my life from corruption, O LORD my God."

Please understand, when he prayed those words, he was praying by faith, not by sight! He prayed those words in the belly of the fish before he was ever delivered. Jonah understood that God's plan for him was to go to Nineveh and preach, and that would require him being brought alive out of the belly of that fish. Jonah was not thanking

God for something that had happened; he was thanking God by faith for something that he knew would happen.

Jonah 2:7 *When my soul fainted within me I remembered the LORD: and my prayer came in unto thee, into thine holy temple.*

Jonah was just about to give up, and he remembered the Lord.

It should never have gotten to that place, by the way. Jonah should never have "forgotten" the Lord. But that forgetting was intentional; it was designed to get out of doing something that Jonah regarded as being unpleasant that God wanted him to do. Once Jonah found the consequences of disobedience more unpleasant than the consequences of obedience, he remembered the Lord and prayed.

Jonah 2:8 *They that observe lying vanities forsake their own mercy.* **9** *But I will sacrifice unto thee with the voice of thanksgiving; I will pay that that I have vowed. Salvation is of the LORD.*

The hinge word between these two verses is the word "but" that begins verse nine. Verse eight and nine are designed as a comparison and contrast.

In verse eight, Jonah spoke of those that observe lying vanities. That phrase is often explained by commentators as being a general reference to those worship idols.

But none of this was "general" in any way. Jonah was not thinking in vague theological terms. The only thing that was on his mind that moment was his own conduct.

Jonah is the one who had "observed lying vanities." Jonah was running from God, less than completely honest with the people who spoke to him about why he was getting on the boat, and very dishonest about his motive when he had them throw him overboard. Jonah had simply not been honest.

But after the chastening hand of God was on him for three days and nights, he said, *They that observe lying vanities forsake their own mercy.*" Jonah had been trying to keep from going to Nineveh for fear that God may extend mercy to the Ninevites, but he finally realized that in his rebellion, all he had done was forsake his own mercy! Jonah had gotten himself into a world of trouble by his own lying vanities.

But Jonah was now determined to be different:

Jonah 2:9 *But I will sacrifice unto thee with the voice of thanksgiving; I will pay that that I have vowed. Salvation is of the LORD.*

We see nothing thankful about Jonah prior to his experience in the fish's belly. Now he is determined to be thankful to God. Now he is determined, in his words, to pay what he has vowed to God.

What would that be? It isn't too hard to figure out. Jonah had been called by God to be a prophet and had accepted that prophetic call. That was always a vow to go where God said to go and to say what God said to say.

Jonah had refused to pay that vow simply because God told him to go to the Ninevites. Now he was ready to pay that vow.

And all of that is what leads to the conclusion of verse nine, a phrase loaded with theological and soteriological implications. The phrase says, "*Salvation is of the LORD.*"

In the context of this verse, Jonah was not talking about his deliverance from the fish's belly. Remember that the verse has been talking about Jonah paying his vow, going to Nineveh, and giving them the word that God tells him to give. In that context, the phrase "salvation is of the Lord" means that Jonah understood that God could extend salvation to whomever He so chooses, including wicked heathen Gentiles like the Ninevites.

This was a huge thing for Jonah and for all of the Jewish people. Even up into the time of Christ and the apostles, there was an incredible reticence on their part to believe that God could and would redeem the Gentiles.

When Peter took the gospel to Cornelius, the Gentile, it caused a huge rift that had to be dealt with in the church in Jerusalem, the first church that was ever officially formed, the church that had been manifestly filled with Holy Ghost power on the day of Pentecost!

Whether it is racial prejudice or the Calvinist's twisted view of redemption, groups of people still imagine that the atonement of God is limited to only a few and that they themselves are somehow that few. They are just like Jonah who believed that the Ninevites were unworthy of the message.

What they cannot seem to grasp is that every last one of us was unworthy of the message and of the offer of salvation, yet, God in His mercy chose to send it to each and every one of us.

Jonah 2:10 *And the LORD spake unto the fish, and it vomited out Jonah upon the dry land.*

There is a character in this whole account that often goes overlooked when we are thinking of individuals that we ought to take pity upon. That character is the fish itself. This creature obeyed its Creator fully. That obedience resulted in its swallowing a live human being. And not just any human being, but a hardheaded, ornery, rebellious, stubborn preacher.

Most of us cannot imagine having that kind of person in our church for three days. Asking any of us to have a person like that in our actual home for three days would be unthinkable. But pity the poor fish who had a preacher like that in his stomach for three days...

This was clearly uncomfortable for Jonah, but it was no picnic for the fish either. This fish was allowed to eat Jonah but was not allowed to digest Jonah. Have you ever had one of those horrible times where you ate something, and it just sat on your stomach and would not digest? That is a horrible feeling. Now imagine if that "something" was still very much alive and was wiggling around in there...

I suspect that the most blessed day of this fish's existence was the day that God told it that it could go to shore and vomit up Jonah. I would suspect the term "projectile vomiting" would hardly be sufficient.

All of this was a study in great will breaking. I cannot conceive of a more stubborn person in all of human history than Jonah. And yet, God was able to break his stubborn will. It would be a wise idea for none of us to put ourselves in a place where it becomes necessary for God to break our stubborn will.

Chapter Eight
A Study In Great Wastefulness

Jonah 3:1 *And the word of the LORD came unto Jonah the second time, saying,* **2** *Arise, go unto Nineveh, that great city, and preach unto it the preaching that I bid thee.* **3** *So Jonah arose, and went unto Nineveh, according to the word of the LORD. Now Nineveh was an exceeding great city of three days' journey.*

The joy and sadness of a second chance

Jonah 3:1 *And the word of the LORD came unto Jonah the second time, saying,* **2** *Arise, go unto Nineveh, that great city, and preach unto it the preaching that I bid thee.*

As we enter the first verses of Jonah 3, we really need to look back at the first couple of verses in chapter one and compare the two passages.

Jonah 1:1 *Now the word of the LORD came unto Jonah the son of Amittai, saying,* **2** *Arise, go to Nineveh, that great city, and cry against it; for their wickedness is come up before me.*

Those two passages are very substantially the same. The first time around, God came to Jonah and said, *"Arise, go unto Nineveh, that great city, and cry against it; for their wickedness is come up before me."*

The second time around, God came to Jonah and said, *"Arise, go unto Nineveh, that great city, and preach unto it the preaching that I bid thee."*

There really is no substantial change. In the first commission of Jonah, God told him to arise and go to Nineveh, and then He gave him the message to preach. In the second commission of Jonah, God once again told him to arise and go to Nineveh, and then He told Jonah to preach what He told him to preach.

In other words, through all of this that had already transpired, God had not changed his mind about anything. But when we move that phrase from generalities into specifics, some beautiful truths emerge.

God had not changed his mind about the wickedness of Nineveh. Time had passed, perhaps even substantial time. And yet the passing days or weeks or months had not altered God's view of the sins of Nineveh.

Had Jonah somehow managed to live one thousand years and run from God all of those thousand years, by the time God finally arrested his attention after those thousand years, His view of the sins of Nineveh still would not have changed one iota. Generations would have come and gone, cultural norms and expectations would have "evolved," as the common vernacular is so fond of saying, but God's views of the sins of Nineveh would still be utterly identical.

When it comes to actual issues of sin, there is simply never going to come a time when sin ceases to be sin in God's sight. Once God declares something a sin, He does not later "undeclared it" a sin.

Mind you, we are not talking about law; we are talking about sin. Certain aspects of the Old Testament law were just that, issues of legality, not issues of morality. Issues of legality may serve a particular time or people group or set of circumstances and later be altered as God sees fit. But issues of morality do not change.

At whatever point God declares an activity to be not just legally forbidden or abominable but specifically morally sinful in His sight, you can be assured that there will never be a revocation of that.

God does not "adapt Himself to the times." He is utterly unchanging and very noticeably so in His Holiness.

If a sin could become an un-sin simply by society changing its views on that activity and God adapting Himself to that change in society's views, then Calvary itself would have been a pointless, empty, and meaningless exercise in futility. If that were the case, all He would have had to do to avoid Calvary is just wait long enough for society's views to evolve to permit and encourage all sin, and then adapt Himself to that change and place every one of all ages underneath that brand-new set of expectations.

But Nineveh was sinful in His sight before Jonah ran, and it was still sinful in His sight after Jonah finally submitted.

No matter how much our society "evolves" to remove the label of unrighteousness from one activity after another, one lifestyle after another, one preference after another, one choice after another, I can assure you on the authority of Scripture that God Himself will not be evolving to go along with those changes in expectation.

This is not a bad thing; it is an excellent thing.

Consider it in the light of a simple sports analogy. Your team, the Wichita Widgets, has somehow made it to the Super Bowl in their very first year of existence. You are ecstatic. You have been pulling for the Widgets since the day they were announced as the newest expansion team of the NFL.

Amazingly, they will be facing the other expansion team that has somehow improbably made it to the Super Bowl, the Catawba Catfish.

The game has been nip and tuck, and the Widgets are down by five points with three seconds left to go in the fourth quarter. Your favorite quarterback, Scam Newtown, drops back to pass, and your best receiver is streaking down the sideline for the end zone. Newtown unloads a long pass, and it is clear that your guy is going to catch it, thus giving your team the Super Bowl win. Then suddenly, a linebacker from the Catfish grabs your receiver by the facemask, yanks him off the ground, spins him around three or four times like some ice skating routine, and flings him off of the field.

You scream, "Facemask!" and pump your fist in celebration because you know your team is about to get the ball on the one-yard line with a chance to punch it in for the win.

But no flag ever comes. You scream at the referee, and you see that your coach is screaming at the referee, both of you are demanding the flag. But the referee calmly says, "You know, previous less enlightened generations considered a facemask to be a violation of the rules. But I have decided to evolve with the times and just let that one slide..."

You would be livid; your team would be livid; every fan of the Widgets would be livid because you played by the long-standing rules, and others didn't. They benefitted unjustly because of the arbitrary change.

So I say again, it is a good thing that God Himself will not be evolving to go along with those changes in moral expectation. Civil law may change, ceremonial law may change, but moral law will never change. Sin will never become un-sin.

God had also, though, not changed His mind about the usefulness of Jonah. And that very thought both amazes and encourages me all at once.

Our view of God so very often is of a hard, unyielding, angry, razor's edge kind of a God just ready to be done with us at the slightest slip. We take his Holiness and somehow confuse it with pettiness; we take His justice and somehow confuse it with an absence of mercy.

But here we have Jonah, who seems to be the textbook example of a person that God would never dream of attempting to use again, and yet here is God renewing the very commission he started with.

Jonah has defied God, disobeyed God, tried to deceive God, tried to destroy himself to avoid serving God, and yet after his repentance, God still views him as useful.

Now please allow me to head off a potential problem at the pass. Having said all that I just said, let me also remind you that Scripture reconciles rather than contradicts itself. I am thinking specifically, as some others probably are at this moment, of the qualifications of the New Testament pastor or deacon.

Jonah was neither of those two things. He was an Old Testament prophet. God Himself gave very specific qualifications for the New Testament pastor or deacon, and those qualifications are inviolable.

People use the example of Jonah, an Old Testament prophet, and often also the example of David, an Old Testament king, and try to conflate those things with the office of a deacon or a pastor. That is akin to trying to make a psychologist and a dentist out to be the same thing:

"Now lean back in your chair, open your mouth very wide. Ahhh, I see you have a cavity. We will need to work on your self-esteem. Repeat after me, 'my cavity is part of me, and I will embrace it... my cavity is part of me, and I will embrace it...' "

One cannot rightly use the example of God's forgiveness and re-commissioning of Jonah to infer that a man who has failed in the qualifications of the New Testament pastor or deacon may still claim a right to those offices. But what we can rightly do is use the example of God's forgiveness and re-commissioning of Jonah to point out that God is way more forgiving than we give Him credit for and willing to use even a great many people that we ourselves would set aside as no longer useful. There are certain things that one can disqualify himself from forever, such as being a pastor or being a deacon.

But anyone who wants to serve God and is willing to repent and return to the God who once called him will find that God is more than willing and more than able to find a way to still use that person.

Anyone can be disqualified from certain things, but no one who repents and returns can be disqualified from everything!

In Jonah's case, he found that nothing he had done disqualified him from fulfilling his purpose. God called him to go to Nineveh and preach the first time, and that same God called him to go and preach to Nineveh a second time.

All of that encompasses the joy of the second chance. But we must, most assuredly, not neglect to mention the sadness of this second chance.

As Jonah stood there on the shore dripping wet and smelling like fish guts, he heard God speak the same words to him that He spoke to him before all of this turmoil took place. Before the storm. Before the being cast overboard. Before the three days and nights in the fish's belly.

God's mind had not changed, but Jonah had changed.

Jonah used to have an unblemished record. Jonah used to be a respected prophet. Jonah used to be able to speak about the judgment of God as something that was going to happen to others. But now Jonah was not just a messenger of God's judgment; he was a living example of it.

Jonah now had to live with the shame and embarrassment of being that guy, the guy that rebelled against God and got swallowed by fish.

Do you realize that if Jonah had obeyed the first time around, we would be speaking about him very differently than we do today? Pay close attention; Jonah literally had the greatest recorded evangelistic campaign in all of human history. Conservatively speaking, well over a million people came to know God through one message that he preached.

But if you walk through Walmart or some other crowded shopping center this afternoon and shout, "Hey! What can anybody here tell me about that guy Jonah from the Bible?" what will everyone instantly mention?

Jonah getting swallowed by the whale. He led the greatest recorded evangelistic campaign in all of human history, conservatively speaking well over a million people came to know God through one message that he preached, and nobody even knows that. All anybody knows about him is that he got swallowed by the great fish.

When you disobey God, even when you repent and later have great results for God, there is always going to be among men the sadness and stigma of your disobedience!

How much better would it be to leave off the sadness part and just have the joy! How much better would it be to do right before God reaches for the paddle.

The journey that resulted in such great waste

Jonah 3:3 *So Jonah arose, and went unto Nineveh, according to the word of the LORD. Now Nineveh was an exceeding great city of three days' journey.*

Not to get too far ahead of ourselves, but once Jonah finally got to Nineveh and preached, everyone there bowed in belief and obedience to God. To put it in our terminology, everyone got saved. Jonah was uniquely gifted by God for this task. He was the man God built for the job, just as surely as the famous fish was the fish that God built for the job. There was not another fish like that one, and there was not another preacher like Jonah.

But though Jonah was uniquely gifted, though Jonah was built for the job, though Jonah was successful, the one thing that cannot be said of Jonah is that he was punctual.

Jonah was late.

Jonah was late by many weeks, maybe even by many months. He went hundreds of miles in the opposite direction, then was carried around the Mediterranean sea for three days and nights, then once he was spat out on dry land, he was still not back even to the starting line.

Let's do some conservative math work. Let's assume Jonah, because of all of this, was just two months late getting to Nineveh. It could have been much more, but I believe two months to be a not unreasonable assumption at the very least. Now let's take a very conservative view of Nineveh of having a population of two million people or so.

The life span in those days was roughly half of what it is today. Today about eight people die per

93

thousand each year, or eight thousand per million. Sixteen thousand per two million. With a lifespan half of ours, therefore, we could expect that in ancient Nineveh, a city of two million people, there would be thirty-two thousand deaths per year. Since the birth rate has always been higher than the death rate, you would not notice a decline in the population, but every year there would be thirty-two thousand new graves or thirty-two thousand cremations. Divide that thirty-two thousand by six to arrive at a two-month span of time you arrive at 5,333 graves that were dug and filled in Nineveh during that two-month interval.

Five thousand three hundred thirty-three. Mothers. Fathers. Sons. Daughters. Brothers. Sisters. Grandparents. Friends.

Jonah's delay resulted in the entire city getting saved, but only those who were still alive to hear the message.

What was it like for a person after the great revival to be walking through town rejoicing in her salvation and then suddenly think of her husband who died a week before Jonah arrived! What was it like for her to weep hot tears and say, "Why, God, why? I am so glad you sent the prophet to me, I am so glad I am going to heaven, but why could the message not have gotten here in time for my husband to hear it?"

Such great, great wastefulness. Jonah was uniquely gifted and specially built and perfectly equipped by God to win the entire city of Nineveh to God, and his diversion into disobedience wasted the precious lives and souls of thousands.

We believers have a responsibility, and so much more. What we actually have is the exact same thing Jonah had: a commission.

Matthew 28:18 *And Jesus came and spake unto them, saying, All power is given unto me in heaven and in earth.* **19** *Go ye therefore, and teach all nations, baptizing them in the name of the Father, and of the Son, and of the Holy Ghost:* **20** *Teaching them to observe all things whatsoever I have commanded you: and, lo, I am with you alway, even unto the end of the world. Amen.*

God has commissioned and equipped us just as He did Jonah. We have everything we need to win souls to God. Jonah delayed for a few weeks or a couple of months. Many of God's people today have delayed far, far longer.

Chapter Nine
A Study in Great Willingness

Jonah 3:4 *And Jonah began to enter into the city a day's journey, and he cried, and said, Yet forty days, and Nineveh shall be overthrown.* **5** *So the people of Nineveh believed God, and proclaimed a fast, and put on sackcloth, from the greatest of them even to the least of them.* **6** *For word came unto the king of Nineveh, and he arose from his throne, and he laid his robe from him, and covered him with sackcloth, and sat in ashes.* **7** *And he caused it to be proclaimed and published through Nineveh by the decree of the king and his nobles, saying, Let neither man nor beast, herd nor flock, taste any thing: let them not feed, nor drink water:* **8** *But let man and beast be covered with sackcloth, and cry mightily unto God: yea, let them turn every one from his evil way, and from the violence that is in their hands.* **9** *Who can tell if God will turn and repent, and turn away from his fierce anger, that we perish not?* **10** *And God saw their works, that they turned from their evil way; and God repented of the evil, that he had said that he would do unto them; and he did it not.*

The limited message of Jonah

Jonah 3:4 *And Jonah began to enter into the city a day's journey, and he cried, and said, Yet forty days, and Nineveh shall be overthrown.*

By this point in the book, God had, on two separate occasions, told Jonah to go and preach to Nineveh. Look again at the two verses where we find those commands:

Jonah 1:2 *Arise, go to Nineveh, that great city, and cry against it; for their wickedness is come up before me.*

Jonah 3:2 *Arise, go unto Nineveh, that great city, and preach unto it the preaching that I bid thee.*

There have been times in this book that we have seen conclusively without a doubt that Jonah disobeyed God. God told Jonah to go to Nineveh; he ran the other direction. That is conclusive disobedience on his part; it cannot be missed. The sailors asked Jonah what they could do to make the sea calm. Rather than tell them to turn the boat around, he told them to throw him overboard. That was conclusive disobedience on his part.

But here we have a case where we are left to sort of guess at whether or not Jonah was fully obedient or only partially obedient.

The beginning call of God to Jonah was for Jonah to go to Nineveh and cry against it because of their wickedness.

Take a look again at the message of Jonah and tell me, did he do that?

Yes, absolutely:

Jonah 3:4 *And Jonah began to enter into the city a day's journey, and he cried, and said, Yet forty days, and Nineveh shall be overthrown.*

God told Jonah to go and cry against the wickedness of Nineveh, and he did that. But look again at the second call of God to Jonah:

Jonah 3:2 *Arise, go unto Nineveh, that great city, and preach unto it the preaching that I bid thee.*

In the second call, God told Jonah to go and preach to Nineveh the preaching "that I bid thee." In other words, there may possibly have been more to the message than just what God told him the first time around.

I am not saying that Jonah disobeyed; I am saying that we do not know if Jonah fully obeyed or not. He may have; he may not have.

But what we do know is this: whether Jonah fully obeyed or just partially obeyed, the message itself was limited. It may have been limited because Jonah did not say everything that God intended for him to say, or it may have been limited because God did not add what we would call "the other part" to it as we would have assumed that He would.

What do I mean by "the other part?"

Jonah delivered a message, but it was only a message of judgment. What would you expect to see that you do not see?

A message of how to avoid that judgment. A message of redemption. A message letting them know how to get right.

Now please do not misunderstand me. God was not obligated to give them that part of the message; in fact, He was not obligated to give them any message at all! But having sent them a message and looking through the rest of the book at how much He clearly loved them and wanted to save them; it really is surprising to only see the message of the coming judgment.

If I stood up in front of lost sinners and preached a scalding message on hell and judgment, what else would you be expecting to hear from me? You would be expecting to hear that that hell and judgment could be avoided by repenting of sin and receiving Christ as Savior.

The Ninevites did not hear anything at all about repenting and getting right; they did not hear anything at all about God wanting to redeem them.

Do you understand how remarkable, therefore, the result of the message was? Without even being told that they could be saved, all of them got saved!

Do not ever, ever, ever underestimate the power of the Word of God! When you and I preach and teach and deliver the Word of God accurately, the most amazing things can happen.

Jonah could have taken a very long time to tell the story of how he was swallowed by a fish. I rather suspect that if I were him, and I had been swallowed by the fish, that when I got there and started preaching a whole lot of my message would be an illustration.

And there is nothing wrong with illustrations. Jesus used a great many illustrations in His preaching. But here was a situation in which a man who could have used a great illustration did not use that illustration, and doing nothing other than delivering God's Word, he saw the most successful evangelistic campaign in all of history.

Jonah could have spent a good while riding his favorite hobby horses, bashing the Ninevites for all of the things the Jews observed that the Assyrians did not. But he just very simply delivered God's word and saw the most successful evangelistic campaign in all of history.

It was only eight words. His entire message was only eight words long.

Have you ever been in a service where a preacher droned on and on so badly and at such lengths that you wished he was preaching an eight-word message?

Jonah preached eight words. That is the epitome of a limited message. And yet, since the message was God's Word, look at the effect that it had.

Pay attention, please, to one other important aspect of this. Jonah's message was a *very negative* message! I have met a surprisingly large number of people, preachers, who take the opinion that all of our messages must be positive. And yet the greatest evangelistic campaign in all of human history was accomplished by the use of a message that was absolutely, thoroughly, completely negative.

Sometimes people do not need to be made to laugh and smile; sometimes they need to be made to weep and mourn. When people are saturated by sin, they do not need to hear a "have your best life now" kind of a message. They need to hear a "sinners in the hands of an angry God" kind of message.

The limitless willingness of Nineveh

Jonah 3:5 *So the people of Nineveh believed God, and proclaimed a fast, and put on sackcloth, from the greatest of them even to the least of them.*

Let me ask what may seem to be an odd question here. We know what Jonah *did* when he got to Nineveh;

he preached. But what did Jonah *not* do when he got to Nineveh?

I know, that is incredibly vague. You could say Jonah did not ride a Ferris wheel; Jonah did not adopt a puppy; Jonah did not knit a blanket; Jonah did not get a tattoo.

But that is not where I am going with this. Jonah just preached, and everybody got saved. So what did Jonah not do that some people in Christian circles say that we have to do if we are going to experience any great results?

Jonah did no miracles. Not one.

Jonah gave no signs. Not one.

All he did was preach. The message was the message.

But without even having to mention himself, in a way, the messenger was also the message.

As we mentioned earlier, one of the deities that the Ninevites worshiped was Dagon, the fish god. And here is a prophet coming through that just so happens to have spent three days and three nights in the belly of the fish and lived to preach anyway.

Just like God directed the plagues on Egypt against the false gods of Egypt, Jonah himself was a message against the false gods of Nineveh.

Look again at the results of the preaching of Jonah:

Jonah 3:5 *So the people of Nineveh believed God, and proclaimed a fast, and put on sackcloth, from the greatest of them even to the least of them.*

They believed. They believed God. Not any of their gods, not Dagon, the real God, the God of the Hebrews.

This verse tells us that they believed, and the very next thing we read is that they *"proclaimed a fast, and put on sackcloth, from the greatest of them even to the least of them."*

Now let me ask you a question at this point, and it should be a very easy one to answer. Is Jesus an expert on salvation and on Scripture and on theology?

Yes.

So, with that in mind, let me read you how Jesus described this:

Matthew 12:41 *The men of Nineveh shall rise in judgment with this generation, and shall condemn it: because they **repented** at the preaching of Jonas; and, behold, a greater than Jonas is here.*

Luke 11:32 *The men of Nineve shall rise up in the judgment with this generation, and shall condemn it: for they **repented** at the preaching of Jonas; and, behold, a greater than Jonas is here.*

The book of Jonah tells us that they *believed* God. Both in the Gospel of Matthew and in the Gospel of Luke, though, Jesus said that they *repented*. It is becoming more and more common these days to hear preachers, whom you think would know better, mock the doctrine of and the need for repentance. Yet here no less an authority than Jesus Himself tied belief and repentance together.

Simply put, there is no such thing as real belief without repentance.

Look at what James said:

James 2:19 *Thou **believest** that there is one God; thou doest well: the devils also **believe**, and tremble.*

Did you realize that the devil is very biblical and Orthodox in his beliefs? The devil believes that Jesus is the Son of God; he was there in heaven to see Him sitting on His throne.

The devil believes that Jesus is virgin born; he knew the prophecy of Isaiah 7:14 well before we did and tried to destroy the baby Jesus in Bethlehem.

The devil believes that Jesus died on the cross; that is where his own head was crushed.

The devil believes that Jesus rose from the dead; the empty tomb was just as available for him to see as anyone else.

The devil "believes" all of the right facts about Jesus. But he has never for a moment repented of his sin and rebellion and bowed his will and heart before Jesus.

Jesus did not say that the Ninevites would condemn this generation for not believing; He said that they would condemn this generation for not repenting.

The Ninevites repented, they *"proclaimed a fast, and put on sackcloth, from the greatest of them even to the least of them."* Everyone, rich or poor, young or old, stopped eating and put sackcloth on, that most visible symbol of a broken heart and a change of mind.

And here is one reason why their belief and repentance was utterly universal:

Jonah 3:6 *For word came unto the king of Nineveh, and he arose from his throne, and he laid his robe from him, and covered him with sackcloth, and sat in ashes.*

We do not conclusively know exactly which of the Assyrian king this was. Some say it was Pul; others, Sardanapalus, others guess that it was Shalmanessar II.

Who it was, though, does not really matter. What really matters is that his example led to everyone else getting right. Because the king was willing to come off of his throne, because he was willing to take off his royal garments, because he was willing to put on sackcloth and sit in ashes, because he was willing to fast, everyone else was willing to humble themselves too.

His repentance led everyone else to repent. We can put it this way; because he stepped out and came down the aisle, everyone else in attendance did so as well.

The most heartbreaking thing imaginable is when one person in a position in a position of influence refuses to bow before Christ in humility, belief, and repentance, and others follow his stubborn lead all the way to hell.

The most wonderful thing imaginable is when a person in a position of influence does bow before Christ in humility, belief, and repentance, and others follow his humble lead all the way to heaven!

When the king repented, look at the proclamation he made:

Jonah 3:7 *And he caused it to be proclaimed and published through Nineveh by the decree of the king and his nobles, saying, Let neither man nor beast, herd nor flock, taste any thing: let them not feed, nor drink water:* **8** *But let man and beast be covered with sackcloth, and cry mightily unto God: yea, let them turn every one from his evil way, and from the violence that is in their hands.*

9 *Who can tell if God will turn and repent, and turn away from his fierce anger, that we perish not?*

There are several things that are striking about his proclamation. One of the first things I notice is that the king did not have to be convinced of the wickedness of himself and his people; verse eight makes it very clear both that he knew they were evil, and he knew the specifics of that evil. Their particular evil of choice, among other things, was violence.

We covered this very early on in our study of the book of Jonah. The Assyrians were legendary for their violence and brutality. So the king of Assyria was not just repenting in a general sense and was not just asking his people to repent in the general sense, he knew that he and they need to very specifically repent of the very specific sin of violence.

That was most assuredly not their only sin, but it was the sin by which they were most marked.

But the more striking thing I notice is that these people repented without even having any kind of a guarantee that it would make a difference. Look at what he said:

"Who can tell if God will turn and repent, and turn away from his fierce anger, that we perish not?"

Who can tell? In other words, he had absolutely no idea if their repentance would make a difference, but he was willing to do it anyway.

How embarrassing is modern man by comparison! The Ninevites were willing to repent even when they had no guarantee that it would make a difference. Modern man is usually unwilling to repent even when he has a rock-solid Biblical guarantee that it will make a difference!

We are talking about the limitless willingness of Nineveh. They were willing to completely prostrate themselves before the God of the Hebrews. They were willing to believe something completely different than they had always been taught. They were willing to repent without any guarantee that it would make a difference.

The lovely repentance of God

Jonah 3:10 *And God saw their works, that they turned from their evil way; and God repented of the evil, that he had said that he would do unto them; and he did it not.*

We have been talking at some length about the repentance of the Ninevites. But they are not the only ones that repented in the book of Jonah. In this verse, we find the lovely repentance of God Himself.

It should go without saying that God never has any sin that He needs to repent of, so His repentance is far different than the repentance of man. When this verse tells us that God repented of the evil that He said He would do unto them, it does not mean evil in the sense of moral wrong; it means evil in the sense of harm and damage. That word is used in that way many times throughout Scripture:

1 Samuel 25:17 *Now therefore know and consider what thou wilt do; for evil is determined against our master, and against all his household: for he is such a son of Belial, that a man cannot speak to him.*

Esther 7:7 *And the king arising from the banquet of wine in his wrath went into the palace garden: and Haman stood up to make request for his life to Esther the queen; for he saw that there was evil determined against him by the king.*

God had determined evil against Nineveh. In fact, it was going to be a very thorough, all-encompassing evil. Nineveh was actually going to be overthrown. But when the Ninevites, one and all, repented of their sin against God, God repented of His determined evil against them.

And this truly is a lovely repentance.

It is lovely in the fact that it was granted to Gentiles, people just like us.

It is lovely in the fact that was granted to one generation even though God knew their descendants just another generation or so down the line would be right back in their sin and rising up against His people.

It was lovely in the fact that God loved them well before they ever loved Him.

It was lovely in the fact that it was utterly undeserved, yet freely given.

What is the book of Jonah? A study in greatness. And here we find a study in great willingness, but really a dual study in great willingness. There was the great willingness of the Ninevites to repent of their sin before God, and there was the great willingness of God to repent of the evil He rightly intended to bring down upon them.

Chapter Ten
A Study in Great Wrong

Jonah 4:1 *But it displeased Jonah exceedingly, and he was very angry.* **2** *And he prayed unto the LORD, and said, I pray thee, O LORD, was not this my saying, when I was yet in my country? Therefore I fled before unto Tarshish: for I knew that thou art a gracious God, and merciful, slow to anger, and of great kindness, and repentest thee of the evil.* **3** *Therefore now, O LORD, take, I beseech thee, my life from me; for it is better for me to die than to live.* **4** *Then said the LORD, Doest thou well to be angry?* **5** *So Jonah went out of the city, and sat on the east side of the city, and there made him a booth, and sat under it in the shadow, till he might see what would become of the city.*

The worst temper-tantrum from a preacher

Jonah 4:1 *But it displeased Jonah exceedingly, and he was very angry.*

This truly is a sad statement to make, but anyone who has been around a great number of preachers for any length of time probably is not surprised by the fact that they are, in fact, capable of throwing temper tantrums, and epic ones at that. But Jonah's temper tantrum in this place is perhaps the most shocking temper tantrum any preacher has ever thrown, mostly because of why he threw it.

If I were to tell you that a preacher threw a temper tantrum over people not responding to a message, I suppose that that would come as no shock at all.

I was on a mission trip a good many years ago, when I encountered what was, to me, the most shocking temper tantrum I had ever seen a preacher throw.

There were several pastors from the United States there on that trip. We were visiting a good many American missionaries in the area and seeing what all was going on in their churches. On the particular visit in question, the missionary had, many weeks previously, asked one of the pastors who would be in attendance to preach on that night. But then, seeing how many people had come, staring wide-eyed at all of the many people in attendance both from the United States and from the field, the missionary chose to "change course."

It was fairly well known that he had not had much in the way of results thus far. Apparently, he was fairly sensitive about that fact and determined to "produce some results" right there on the spot in order to impress the American pastors and gain more support.

Rather than calling the scheduled pastor up to preach, he began to preach himself off the cuff, extemporaneously. As the pastor of that mission field church, he certainly had the right to do so, that was not the problem at all. The problem was that he preached what he believed to be a scalding, powerful salvation message, designed to instill in everyone the fear of hell and the knowledge that most of them were probably themselves going to that awful place.

When I say that everyone there was unmoved, I mean "unmoved like wooden Indians." There simply was no power in anything that was happening. There was a lot of volume, a lot of yelling, and finally, all of it reached a screaming crescendo of an invitation. The man demanded that everyone recognize their lost estate and come to the altar at once. Mind you, he was dealing with people who not only were saved but were under such a burden for souls that they themselves were visiting the mission field to see how they could help.

No one came to the altar.

Turning red in the face, he began to shriek in tones that would make a demon-possessed witch turn green with envy.

No one came to the altar.

He began to threaten that he was sure, quite sure, God had given him a word there were lost people in attendance, and that this was their very last chance to ever be born again.

No one came to the altar.

Things had been going on for over an hour, and the only movement was people squirming uncomfortably, wondering when he would be done.

Finally, he hit upon a brilliant tactic to convince us all to come to the altar. He took his belt off, and my eyebrows along with everyone else's went up, wondering if he was about to end up badly beaten and in the hospital as a result of having tried to physically spank people into coming to the altar.

But that was not it. He went to the back door of the church, laid his belt across the threshold, and said, "If you are 100% sure that you are born again, you may cross over this belt and leave the church. But be aware that if you cross this belt in your lost estate, God will never again give you a chance to be saved, and you will die and go to hell for all eternity!"

I was the first one across the belt and out the door. I did not look back or even slow down until I was at least a quarter of a mile down the road and away from the church. When I finally stopped and turned around, I could not help but giggle; I looked like Moses leading the children of Israel out of Egypt! There was a mass exodus following me heading for the Promised Land, which at that moment was anywhere other than that church.

And in the distance, I could hear Pharaoh, I mean that missionary, shrieking at the top of his lungs, "All you people get back here and get back across this belt and down to this altar!"

No dice, Bud, no dice.

That was an epic temper tantrum over people not "getting saved." But it is not even close to the epic and dramatic nature of the temper tantrum that Jonah threw, because Jonah did not throw a temper tantrum over people *not* getting saved, Jonah threw a temper tantrum because everyone *did* get saved! Verse one tells us that it "*displeased Jonah exceedingly, and he was very angry.*"

Can you imagine the lunacy, the twisted irony of a preacher being so powerful in his preaching that more than a million people get saved all at the same time, and his reaction being "exceedingly displeased and very angry."

I have known preachers to get angry when multitudes were saved under someone else's preaching because they were jealous that they themselves were not doing much, but I have never in all my years known of a preacher getting angry over multitudes of people getting saved at his own preaching!

It seems that between the walk from the seashore where the fish spit him out and the midst of Nineveh where he ended up, Jonah once again chose to lose sight of the fact that "salvation is of the Lord."

While Jonah was in the fish's belly, God managed to humble him to the point where he was willing to let God be God and save whomever He wanted to save, even if it was the violent Gentile Ninevites. But once Jonah was out on dry land and was able to "walk it off," his old hatred and prejudice returned full force.

He obeyed, but he obeyed hoping for no results.

He preached, but he preached hoping for the message to fall on deaf ears and hardened hearts.

And when he found himself successful in the task to which the Lord had sent him, he was "exceedingly displeased and very angry."

The worst testimony from a preacher

Jonah 4:2 *And he prayed unto the LORD, and said, I pray thee, O LORD, was not this my saying, when I was yet in my country? Therefore I fled before unto Tarshish: for I knew that thou art a gracious God, and* *merciful, slow to anger, and of great kindness, and repentest thee of the evil.* **3** *Therefore now, O LORD, take, I beseech thee, my life from me; for it is better for me to die than to live.*

Verse two opens a window into the past for us and makes us privy to a conversation that Jonah had with God before he ever made the horrible decision to attempt to run from God. It says, *"O LORD, was not this my saying, when I was yet in my country?"*

He is referring to the fact that the Ninevites repented and got saved. He is reminding God that he told God this would happen. In other words, before Jonah ran for Tarshish, something like this happened:

"Jonah?"

"LORD, is that you?"

"Yes, Jonah, it is."

"Speak, Lord, for thy servant heareth."

"Good, Jonah. Here, then, is what I have to say to you. Jonah, I need you to fulfill your office as a prophet. I need you to go and speak a word in my name."

"Yes, Lord, whatever you say I will do. Shall I go back to King Jereboam and speak to him once again, is that what you desire of me? Or would you like me to stand in the midst of the city and cry against the sins of your people, Israel, and warn them to repent?"

"No, Jonah, neither of those things. I need you to go much farther afield. Jonah, arise, go to Nineveh, the capital city of Assyria, and cry against it, for their wickedness is come up before me."

"But Lord! Nineveh and the Ninevites are horrible! God, they hate You and all Your people. They are brutal

114

and bloodthirsty, and as soon as they get the smallest chance, they will not hesitate to destroy us!"

"Did I not say that they were wicked? You have just confirmed that. So do as I have said; go and cry against their wickedness."

"But Lord, that isn't the point. The point is, if I go and cry against their wickedness, they will repent. And I know You; You are gracious and merciful, slow to anger, and of great kindness, and often turn away from the destruction You plan to bring down on people. If they repent, You will forgive them rather than destroy them!"

And so Jonah ran. He ran toward Tarshish, ended up in Nineveh anyway, preached, and exactly what he feared would happen did happen. And when it did, Jonah said:

Jonah 4:3 *Therefore now, O LORD, take, I beseech thee, my life from me; for it is better for me to die than to live.*

Jonah literally became suicidal over his success! Jonah had all the right head knowledge, all the right words, and all the wrong spirit. He knew God so very well that he knew exactly how He would react in a given situation, and yet he knew so very little of the heartbeat of God that he felt completely different about it than God felt about it.

That is a terrible testimony from a preacher or from any child of God. How could any of us have so much head knowledge of God, be able to utter such an accurate testimony of God, and yet be pulling in such a different direction than God?

115

The worst tuning out of a preacher

Jonah 4:4 *Then said the LORD, Doest thou well to be angry?* **5** *So Jonah went out of the city, and sat on the east side of the city, and there made him a booth, and sat under it in the shadow, till he might see what would become of the city.*

Jonah has just thrown a royal, epic temper tantrum. He has just demonstrated the worst imaginable testimony for a preacher or even for just a random child of God. And when God spoke to him about that, notice how many words He said to him:

Six.

What Jonah had done was so clearly and egregiously in the wrong, that there was absolutely no need for a long lecture explaining how and why it was wrong. God simply said, "Doest thou well to be angry?"

When God can deliver His entire corrective message to you in six very small words, you have really messed up. And when you have really messed up, and God comes to you with a simple straightforward message of correction, what should your response be?

Definitely not this:

Jonah 4:5 *So Jonah went out of the city, and sat on the east side of the city, and there made him a booth, and sat under it in the shadow, till he might see what would become of the city.*

No repentance. No apology. Not even a response. God spoke to Jonah, and Jonah simply turned away from Him and walked off. He left the city and made himself a comfortable place to sit so that he could see what would happen to the city, hoping that God would finally "see

116

things his way" and go ahead and destroy the city anyway. He wanted God to revoke the redemption of those who had repented at his preaching.

In recent years it has become somewhat fashionable among some preachers to try and redeem the image of Jonah. But at least in this instance, there really is no honest way to do so. This was not just wrong; it was great wrong. And it was great wrong from a person who knew God enough to have known better.

Chapter Eleven
A Study in Great Worthiness

Jonah 4:6 *And the LORD God prepared a gourd, and made it to come up over Jonah, that it might be a shadow over his head, to deliver him from his grief. So Jonah was exceeding glad of the gourd.* **7** *But God prepared a worm when the morning rose the next day, and it smote the gourd that it withered.* **8** *And it came to pass, when the sun did arise, that God prepared a vehement east wind; and the sun beat upon the head of Jonah, that he fainted, and wished in himself to die, and said, It is better for me to die than to live.* **9** *And God said to Jonah, Doest thou well to be angry for the gourd? And he said, I do well to be angry, even unto death.* **10** *Then said the LORD, Thou hast had pity on the gourd, for the which thou hast not laboured, neither madest it grow; which came up in a night, and perished in a night:* **11** *And should not I spare Nineveh, that great city, wherein are more than sixscore thousand persons that cannot discern between their right hand and their left hand; and also much cattle?*

A powerful object lesson

Jonah 4:6 *And the LORD God prepared a gourd, and made it to come up over Jonah, that it might be a shadow over his head, to deliver him from his grief. So Jonah was exceeding glad of the gourd.* **7** *But God prepared a worm when the morning rose the next day, and it smote the gourd that it withered.* **8** *And it came to pass, when the sun did arise, that God prepared a vehement east wind; and the sun beat upon the head of Jonah, that he fainted, and wished in himself to die, and said, It is better for me to die than to live.*

We ended the last lesson with Jonah storming out of the city, completely ignoring God's question to him:

Jonah 4:5 *So Jonah went out of the city, and sat on the east side of the city, and there made him a booth, and sat under it in the shadow, till he might see what would become of the city.*

No repentance. No apology. Not even a response. God spoke to Jonah, and Jonah simply turned away from Him and walked off. He left the city and made himself a comfortable place to sit so that he could see what would happen to the city, hoping that God would finally "see things his way" and go ahead and destroy the city anyway. He wanted God to revoke the redemption of those who had repented at his preaching.

What this tells us is that it was still within the forty-day period that Jonah had preached about. Jonah had seen the incredible repentance of the Ninevites.

And he assumed (correctly) that God was going to rescind His planned destruction of them.

But just in case, Jonah went outside the city to sit and wait and watch.

What should Jonah have been doing? Clearly, he should have been discipling them, helping them to grow in their walk with the Lord, praying and fasting for them, shepherding them.

But instead, he is silently watching, hoping for their destruction. And he has made a little booth to sit under to somewhat shield himself from the brutal desert sun as he sits and watches.

As we pick things up in verse six, we find God showing great mercy again, this time to Jonah:

Jonah 4:6 *And the LORD God prepared a gourd, and made it to come up over Jonah, that it might be a shadow over his head, to deliver him from his grief. So Jonah was exceeding glad of the gourd.*

What Jonah did was not enough of a shadow. His little booth, hastily thrown together, was no match for the brutal heat of the desert. So God, once again in this book, "prepared" something very out of the ordinary. As Jonah sat sweating under his little booth, a little sprout stuck its head up out of the ground. In amazement, Jonah noticed that he could actually see it growing! It not only grew; it did so as if by design. It literally wove itself together and did so so very tightly that within an incredibly short span of time it had formed a living canopy over Jonah. God had done a miracle in preparing this gourd for him.

And look specifically at why He did it: to deliver Jonah from his what? Grief. His grief. Jonah was literally *grieving* over the salvation of the Ninevites! When we think of grief, the funeral of a loved one immediately comes to mind. This was Jonah's frame of mind; the Ninevites getting saved made him feel like his own mother just died.

He was being stupid and wrong, yes; but God did something to soothe his grief anyway! How good and how gracious is our God?

Jonah, for his part, was "exceeding glad" of it. It was just a gourd, just a plant growing from the ground, but Jonah loved it because it made him feel better physically.

But God's ultimate goal in preparing this gourd was not to soothe Jonah's grief; He had something much bigger in mind.

Jonah 4:7 *But God prepared a worm when the morning rose the next day, and it smote the gourd that it withered.*

There is the third time in the book we find God "preparing" something very out of the ordinary. He prepared a fish, He prepared a gourd, and now He prepared a worm.

A worm. Singular. Think of how strong and vibrant this vine and gourd was; it grew and overshadowed Jonah, it made a canopy for him in just a matter of minutes.

And yet one prepared worm wiped it out in a day.

But things were about to get worse:

Jonah 4:8 *And it came to pass, when the sun did arise, that God prepared a vehement east wind; and the sun beat upon the head of Jonah, that he fainted, and wished in himself to die, and said, It is better for me to die than to live.*

This is the fourth thing God prepared in this book. He prepared a fish, He prepared a gourd, He prepared a worm, and now He has prepared a "vehement east wind."

The shadow is gone. And between the sun and the wind, Jonah feels like he is in a blast furnace. *He feels like he is undergoing the judgement of God...*

It is so bad that he wants to die. He is miserable.

Do you see the object lesson? The Ninevites had grown strong. The gourd had grown strong. God said he would destroy the Ninevites, and Jonah was happy; he wanted them destroyed. God did destroy the gourd, and Jonah was unhappy. He did not want it destroyed. The Ninevites were of no use to Jonah, the gourd was. This was all about Jonah! Everything centered around Jonah.

Jonah wanted the Ninevites to feel the hot judgment of God, but he did not want to feel the much smaller judgment of a hot wind.

Everything about Jonah was out of whack, and God was giving him a visual illustration to help him figure that out.

But it was not working. At the end of verse eight, we find him wallowing in self-pity rather than repenting of his horrible attitude.

A petulant prophet

Jonah 4:9 *And God said to Jonah, Doest thou well to be angry for the gourd? And he said, I do well to be angry, even unto death.*

Rewind back to the moment right before Jonah left the city:

Jonah 4:4 *Then said the LORD, Doest thou well to be angry?*

What should Jonah's answer have been to that six-word question? *No, Lord, I do not...*

But instead, he stormed off. So, since Jonah could not seem to grasp the big picture, God painted a smaller one for him. A gourd grew. A plant. Not a human. And when it was destroyed, Jonah was heart-sick.

Then God asked the exact same question he asked before, with three added words:

Jonah 4:9 *And God said to Jonah, Doest thou well to be angry **for the gourd**?*

When God asked the question the first time, what did Jonah say? Nothing.

But now he suddenly becomes very talkative:

Jonah 4:9b *...and he said, I do well to be angry, even unto death.*

Really? Over being hot?

That is some serious petulance; there is no way to spin that positively.

A perfect God

Jonah 4:10 *Then said the LORD, Thou hast had pity on the gourd, for the which thou hast not laboured, neither madest it grow; which came up in a night, and perished in a night: 11 And should not I spare Nineveh, that great city, wherein are more than sixscore thousand persons that cannot discern between their right hand and their left hand; and also much cattle?*

Jonah had, here is the word, "pity" on the gourd. You can almost see Jonah gasping when he realized what the worm was doing, and trying to get hold of that creature and keep it from killing the gourd. You can almost see Jonah running around looking for water for the plant, hoping that will help. You can almost hear him talking to the plant, *"Don't die, little plant, hang in there, you are special, God loves you, and I need you!"*

But the plant died. And when Jonah complained, God reminded Jonah that he had done literally *nothing* to get that gourd. God did it; God did it all. That was God's gourd, growing out of God's ground, being hydrated by God's water, and energized by God's sun all for God's purposes.

God then reminded Jonah that this gourd was so very temporary and not of much worth.

It was a plant. A plant!

Then God dropped the hammer:

Jonah 4:11 *And should not I spare Nineveh, that great city, wherein are more than sixscore thousand persons that cannot discern between their right hand and their left hand; and also much cattle?*

"You are very concerned about a plant dying, Jonah. But what about that old grandmother down on First Street there in Nineveh? She was about to die and go to hell; does she not matter? What about the group of kids playing in the park? Are you okay with them being destroyed? Really, Jonah?"

And yet notice that there is no verse twelve. Where is the verse twelve that should be here? Where is the verse that should end this book saying, "And Jonah bowed before the Lord, fully understanding his wretchedness, and repented."

It is not there. There is no verse twelve.

If you have somehow become a Jonah, may I ask you, please, to do something?

Right now, this very moment, make sure there is a verse twelve in your life.

Works Cited

Feinberg, Charles. *The Minor Prophets*. Chicago: Moody
    Press, 1976.

Mark, Joshua J. "Assyrian Warfare"
    https://www.ancient.eu/Assyrian_ Warfare/,
    (accessed Ocotber 2019)

Poole, Matthew. *Matthew Poole's Commentary*.
    https://biblehub.com/commentaries/poole/jonah/1.
    htm, (accessed October 2019)

Other Books by Dr. Bo Wagner

Book Series
Daniel: Breathtaking
Esther: Five Feast and the Finger Prints of God
James: The Pen and the Plumb Line
Nehemiah: A Labor of Love
Romans: Salvation From A-Z
Ruth: Diamonds in the Darkness

Beyond the Colored Coat
Don't Muzzle the Ox
From Footers to Finish Nails
I'm Saved! Now What???
Learning Not to Fear the Old Testament
Marriage Makers, Marriage Breakers

The Night Heroes Series:
Cry From the Coal Mine (Vol. 1)
Free Fall (Vol. 2)
Broken Brotherhood (Vol. 3)
The Blade of Black Crow (Vol. 4)
Ghost Ship (Vol. 5)
When Serpents Rise (Vol. 6)
Moth Man (Vol. 7)
Runaway (Vol. 8)

Zak Blue and the Great Space Chase:
Falcon Wing (Vol. 1)

www.ingramcontent.com/pod-product-compliance
Lightning Source LLC
Chambersburg PA
CBHW072025040426
42447CB00009B/1738